Other books by Leonard M. Foley, IIII:

THINGS TO THINK ABOUT

THE BOOK OF BLAH, BLAH, BLAH*

THE RIDICULOUS WISDOM OF
RUPERT BUMPKIN*

IF GOD IS DEAD, WHY DO I
FEEL SO ALIVE?

GOD IS HIDDEN TO THOSE
WHO HIDE*

THE FOOL'S GUIDE TO A
HAPPY LIFE*

ON YOUR MARK, GET SET,
WAKE UP!*

*To be published by ONE WORLD PUBLISHING
December 1997

"We all need a little
madness to keep from
going insane!"

Dedicated to the Crazy-Masters
of the world. May their madness set
us all free.

An original publication of ONE WORLD PUBLISHING™
First trade hardback in April 1996

Cartoons by: Mark Hentemann*

© Copyright 1996 Leonard M. Foley, III

All rights reserved.

International Standard Book No. 0-9630314

Library of Congress Catalog
Card Number: 96-092153

1   2   3   4   5   6   7   8   9   10

*Mark Hentemann can be
 contacted at:
 2761 Euklid Heights Blvd.
 Apt. # 2
 Cleveland Heights, Ohio
 44106

Distributed by:

New Leaf Distribution Co.
401 Thornton Rd.
Lithia Springs, GA 30057
1-800-326-2665

Devorss & Company
P.O Box 550
Marina Del Rey, CA 90294
1-800-843-5743

Baker & Taylor Books
44 Kirby Ave.
Sommerville, NJ 08876
1-800-775-1500

AN INTRODUCTION TO INSANITY...

When was the last time you did something a little crazy? Something sudden, spontaneous and free? Can you think of something recent? Perhaps in the last few days? If you can't think of anything just yet, don't despair. The simple action of having purchased this book puts you off to a fairly good start.

This is a book about your freedom. Freedom to do what you want when you want to do it. It is about becoming a Crazy-Master of your life. A Crazy-Creator of your own destiny. It is not written for the sensible, rational fear mongers who live by the ultra-cautious dictums of common sense----this book takes common sense and turns it on its ear! It takes everything most people hold as sacred and revered and transforms it into a cosmic paradox of possibilities.

6

Most people are going to think you're crazy for reading this book because most people don't think like the Crazy-Master. And *who* is the Crazy-Master? He is not what most humdrummers think he is. He is not crazy in the clinical sense of the word, he is crazy in the liberating sense. He is not "inflicted" with the sickness of madness he *chooses to dance in the glory of it.*

Madness for the Crazy-Master is not a dis-ease of the mind it is an at-ease of the heart. The Crazy-Master is happier, healthier, and more joyous than most of his humdrum contemporaries. He is different from the rest of the world because he doesn't care what anyone else thinks of his behavior. He has a joyous calm in knowing that he is free from the influences of the infectious crowd and celebrates his uniqueness by enjoying himself with amazing alacrity and delight.

There are not enough Crazy-Masters in this world. And it is my hope that this book might create a few more. Have fun with this material.

It is an invitation to your Crazy-Master freedom. Read what appeals to you now and skip over the rest. Perhaps the spirit of Crazy-Wisdom will inspire you to return to it at a later date. For now it is not important *what* or *how much* you read---it is only important that you embrace a few of the Crazy-Master principles as an alternate way for you to experience and engage your life.

This book begins as an instruction manual and ends up as an inspirational guide. I don't recommend that you read the last few sections without first perusing a few of the introductory chapters. There is a method to this madness and the method is madness itself.

Horace wrote, "a pleasant madness inspires me" and these pages are your first step to experiencing the Crazy-Master inspiration of unencumbered madness and delight. We all need a little madness to keep from going insane and this book shows you how to do it. Read these words as though your mental and psychological health depended upon them, because from the perspective of the Crazy-Master---they do.

May your madness set you free!

Len Toby

"I don't want to go among
mad people,"
Alice remarked.
"Oh, you can't help that,"
said the Cat:
"we're all mad here.
I'm mad. You're mad."
-Lewis Carroll
<u>Alice in Wonderland</u>

PART ONE:

The Teachings
Of The Crazy-Master

1. THE INSANE GUIDE TO FEARLESSNESS...

The Crazy-Master must be weird if he is going to be crazy and must be crazy if he is going to be a Master. Weirdness is as normal to the Crazy-Master as humdrum normalness is to you or me.

The Crazy-Master does not fear the potential humiliation of appearing a bit eccentric to the outside world. After all, what could be better than being known for doing things a bit differently from the crowd? Humiliation is a blessing to the Crazy-Master because it is a constant reminder of his desire to live his life in an original and unique way.

Think about it, how many people who laughed at the Crazy-Master in high school are around to laugh at him today? In the long run, no one is really going to care about how the Crazy-Master chooses to live his life. Are there really any

11

people so pathetically bored with their own lives that they actually have the time to scrutinize and evaluate the lives of others? If so, God help them! There is no greater critic in life than those obtuse, blunted shlumps who have no lives of their own.

Oh! he is mad, is he? Then I wish he would bite some other of my generals.
-George II of Great Britain
-Reply to one who complained that General Wolfe was a madman

The bottom line is, no matter what choice the Crazy-Master makes with his life, there will inevitably be someone *somewhere* who will gladly laugh at him and scorn his decision. So I say forget about other people's opinions. Shrug them off like the pesky insects they are and allow the Crazy-Master within to make the choices that bring true happiness and joy. Life is too short and uninformed opinions are too long. The

Crazy-Master doesn't worry about what his neighbors are saying. If they were *really* happy with their own choices then they'd be too interested in themselves to even care about the choices of anyone else.

> *That so few now dare to be eccentric, marks the chief danger of our time.*
> -John Stuart Mill

Fearlessness takes practice...

It takes time to become an autonomous abnormality. You may have to start out small, perhaps adorning a ridiculous tie at the office or wearing silly clown shoes to a formal event. The key is in stretching your boundaries of humiliation. Trying new things that stir up the emotional pot around you and then see how you respond. If you become embarrassed and blush wildly with your initial attempts then you are trying too hard---doing too much. Your actions should be small enough to be handled gracefully, in a detached, un-flustered position of strength.

Eventually, outrageousness and shocking behavior can be easily experienced and even enjoyed---but not until the requisite emotional preparation is under your belt. Watch how you respond to the little things. See if you immediately make apologies for your actions that don't fit into accepted social rubrics. Watch for unconscious excuses you may give to yourself for not going all out in certain social circumstances.

A novice in the area of crazy-wisdom who tries to become too shocking and too outrageous without the necessary psychological groundwork may become so humiliated and emotionally damaged that he is hesitant and fearful to try anything else. That is why at first, small steps are so important. They teach the budding Master how to handle mockery and respond to ridicule. It provides him with a level of detachment that enables him to move into any area of his life with confidence and unfettered power.

A little madness in the spring
Is wholesome even for the King.
-Emily Dickinson

2. THE INSANE GUIDE TO SUCCESS...

If the Crazy-Master wants to become successful he must first become successfully abnormal. Successful people aren't necessarily the smartest or hardest working people in the world---they are the most abnormal. Look at any successful person, did he get that way doing the same things as everyone else? Did he achieve greatness by following the status quo?

Vincent Van Gogh, regarded by most of his contemporaries as a lunatic and a freak, was one of the most abnormally successful painters of all time. Did he become successful by following the established painting techniques of his day? Absolutely not! Van Gogh was years ahead of his time. His work was beyond anything anyone had ever seen. He sold only one painting during his lifetime. And that was to his brother, Theo. He didn't paint because of money (he died penniless) or because of fame (he lived in obscurity)---he painted because it made sense for him to do so. He painted because it was what his interior abnormality directed him to do.

> *No great genius has ever existed without some touch of madness.*
> *-Aristotle*

Where is your interior abnormality ?

Do you like to dance? Do you like to bake? Draw? Sing? Write poetry? Walk around the house naked? What is it that makes sense for you to do, even though it may make you look a little weird to the outside world? The challenge of abnormality is to release these feelings of weirdness. To awaken the weirdo within and embrace your abnormality with energetic delight.

Van Gogh was abnormal because he chose to move beyond the norm. What is your norm? What are your comfort zones that need dilation? Can you face the consequences of your uniqueness? Can you endure the possible alienation and estrangement from your family and friends?   Originality can do this to you. It can place you miles apart from the ordinary crowd and worlds apart from the crowd's ordinary thinking. There is nothing so debilitating to our originality than being thought of as weird or strange in the eyes of our friends, co-workers, family and even ourselves---but----in the world of abnormal insanity that is a consequence every Crazy-Master must be willing to face.

The world has always gone through periods of madness so as to advance a bit on the road to reason.
-Hermann Broch

Suggestions for successful abnormality...

Do you want to become successful? Do you want to win in the market place? In your particular enterprise? With your particular product? Then do what other people aren't doing.

17

If "everyone" is selling red socks, sell blue. If "everyone" puts their labels on right side up, put yours on upside down. If "everyone" advertises in your local newspaper, hire a banner plane instead.

The really sane man knows he has a touch of the madman, the madman is quite sure he is sane.
-G.K. Chesterton

The key here is not to *compete* but to *create!* Anyone can imitate---but as a Crazy-Master you must learn to *innovate.* Create your own uniqueness and watch your competition disappear! There is no competitive pressure for the Crazy-minded-Master because his directions are always uncharted and unusual. He is invariably the most successful person in any field because he is usually the only one there.

Steve Jobs, the founder of Apple Computer, is a prime example. When he first brought his ideas to the market, the products that he produced were the only one of their kind in the arena. His nearest competitors were miles away still *competing.* Jobs knew he couldn't challenge IBM on their own turf so he went out and *created* his own.

> *Blest madman, who could*
> *every hour employ,*
> *With something new to wish,*
> *or to enjoy.*
> *-John Dryden*

Your own abnormality...

Have you heard about the unemployed college graduate who was in desperate need of a job? He did all of the "expected" things that college grads were supposed to do. He distributed resumes, went on interviews, and "networked" with various alumni groups. He even tapped into a few family connections for work---but no matter how persistent he was in his "expected practices"---he still found no job.

Finally, out of Crazy-Master desperation, he did something out of the ordinary---he went to the busiest street corner in his city, and in one hand he held up a large sign that read, *"Unemployed college grad in search of job. Hard-working and ambitious.*" In his other hand he had a stack of resumes that he passed out to anyone who would take one. His antics got him on the front page of the city's largest newspaper and he had a list of phone messages from prospective employers within a few hours. Three days later he had the job of his choice.

If insanity is defined as a deviation from the psychological norm, the divine madman is truly crazy, but if a spiritual ideal is used as a yard stick, undoubtedly, it is the vast majority of us who are insane.
-Keith Dowman

There was another young man who was repeatedly rejected by a list of mediocre advertising agencies in his home town. Frustrated, but not defeated he decided to try something a bit different. He made a four and a half square foot resume! He sent it to one of the countries largest Ad agencies with a note that read "Now that I've got your attention, please read my resume! I will do whatever it takes to work for your company." They called him the next day and within two weeks he had a job.

He who lives without folly is not so wise as he imagines.
-Rochefoucauld

There are innumerable ways to make your abnormal uniqueness known. And all it takes is just a little creative imagination to make it happen.

Imagine the pain of not having tried something that may have paid off with enormous possibilities of happiness and fulfillment? What could be more painful than looking back upon your life with the complaint, "If only I did this or that..." Don't join the humdrum death squad! Do what makes you happy! Even if you have to look a little ridiculous in the process---it is worth it in the end.

We reclaim ourselves with precocious insanity, with blazing madness, with tenacious cannibalism. Accommodate yourselves to me. I do not accommodate myself to you.
-Aimé Césaire

3. THE INSANE GUIDE TO "EVERYONE"...

A Crazy-Master is always original. He is not concerned with what "everyone" is doing because what "everyone" does is usually nothing worth doing. If there is a movement of the crowd, the Crazy-Master is never behind it or within it, but usually you can find him *above* it---dropping down water balloons or some other devious device to shock them out of their apathetic trudge into nowhere.

For example, if "everyone" is spending $20,000 per year on a four year education---the Crazy-Master might take two years off and buy himself $1,000 worth of books and educational movies. (he'll save himself $39,000 worth of excessive course work, have plenty of free time to study the things he *really* loves, and have an impressive library to boot.)

If "everyone" takes the elevator---the Crazy-Master will take the stairs. If "everyone" walks forward---the Crazy-Master will walk backwards. If "everyone" eats ice cream and apple pie---the Crazy-Master will eat broccoli and chocolate cake. If "everyone" believes in aliens from other planets---the Crazy-Master will believe he's one of them!

Either I must be mad or everyone else is; there are no two ways about it.
-Vimalananda

Where is your originality?

Do you want to do things differently than your parents, friends and siblings? Do you want an original life? A creative existence that is unique to yourself?

If your answer is "yes"---then your answer is to be yourself. In fact, the only way to be original is to be yourself because *your* self is the only original self you've got.

What contribution can you make being someone else? Most young people think they are rebelling against the status quo. They believe they are being "original" and "unique". But have you ever taken a look at these "originals"? They look just like every other "original" that is supposedly rebelling against the status quo! In fact, if you put all these "originals" together in a room it would be hard to tell them apart.

Originality has nothing to do with most of the things "normal" people do to appear unique. It has nothing to do with fancy haircuts, new cars, or fancy dress.

Originality comes from within. It is the attitude with which you confront the circumstances of your life. It is awakening each day with a renewed sense of wonder and hope, embracing every circumstance as your teacher and guide.

Originality is your acceptance of reality and those things which reality brings. In essence, originality is doing the things that 95% of the humdrum people never do! It is living life with gratitude, joy and a sense of purpose for your existence.

Originality can make you great but it is not without a great price. It will cost you a lot to be yourself. It may even cost you the self you already think you are.

The true madman is
God.
-Baul expression

Don't back down to "everyone"..

The humdrum crowd will do anything in its power to thwart your creative uniqueness. If you decide to take dance lessons or harmonica classes you will hear things like, "You're going to spend $50 a week on what??? It's too frivolous! Invest in mutual funds instead..." Don't listen to such nonsense! If it's what you want it is worth whatever price you can afford. You can't put a price-tag on happiness and personal fulfillment. But when you're miserable and dissatisfied with your choices, no price will be enough.

The humdrum crowd will mock you for your initial efforts of originality because it fears any actions that shake up its hypnotic indifference. It will not understand why you are doing things so differently from the norm and will angrily confront you at every step. Again, do not be dismayed. It is part of the Crazy-Master process. There just aren't many of us around and because we are in the minority we will always seem a bit odd to the mass of people living their lives asleep.

Insanity is a matter

of degree.
-Joaquim Machado De Assis

4. THE INSANE GUIDE TO THE WEIRDO WITHIN...

Everyone has a weirdo within. We can try and candy coat it with fancy names and elevate it with elaborate platitudes, but when it comes right down to it, lurking deep within us all, lies this enigmatic force that is just plain strange.

Most people attach great value to the virtue of soulful living but ascribe very little or no value to the virtue of soulful weirdness. For example, look at any of the great mystics and saints throughout the history of the world. What is the one thing they all had in common? Was it their holiness? It depends on the cultural context. What makes one mystic similar to another if their beliefs and ideals are world's apart? They all have one thing in common. It is something universal to any one touched by the spirit of our

Crazy Creator: they have all found and befriended their hidden *weirdo* within.

Fools and madmen tell commonly truth.
-Robert Burton

Whenever I tell this to someone who is particularly rigid in his religious thought, the common response is one of disbelief. "How can you call God's chosen messengers weirdoes? You are blaspheming against our Holy Creator!" My response is usually the same: I refer him to the life of one of the greatest weirdo soul-searchers of all time---St. Francis of Assisi, (who's incredible strangeness, incidentally, endeared him to virtually everyone he came into contact with). I point out the fact that St. Francis very often preached naked to the masses. He spent time talking with animals and is even rumored to have converted a goat to Christianity! He offended many people with his weirdness and

29

yet historically he is one of the finest examples of holy discipleship we have ever seen.

We are all born mad,

some remain so.
-Samuel Beckett

St. Francis was a great saint because he was comfortable being weird. He didn't care what other people thought of him and that is the secret to his greatness. He did his thing his own way. He didn't consult his neighbor's opinion for his own personal validation---he consulted his heart and found validation knowing what was right for himself to do---and then going fearlessly ahead and doing it.

Each time he thought that he was mad, he met someone else with a head full of sane, socially acceptable madness.
-Richard Wright
<u>The Outsiders</u>

Befriending the weirdo within...

Where is *your* weirdo within? What crazy antics is it directing for you? Do you want to travel throughout Europe with a backpack and sketch pad? Do you want to travel across China on a motorcycle? Do you want to share your outrageous religious faith with the rest of the world? Do you want freedom from your job? From your school? From your restrictive circle of acquaintances?

What does the weirdo within want you to do? Maybe it wants you to find a quiet retreat one day each week in the mountains. Maybe it wants you to audition for the circus or join a traveling theater company. Maybe it wants you to be freed from the laughter and scorn of other people.

The weirdo within is diligent in its demands and persistent in its rewards. If you are fearful about being weird then you are fearful about life itself---and as any Crazy-Master will tell you, it is *life* itself that makes us feel so weird.

When we remember we are all mad, the mysteries disappear and life stands explained.
-Mark Twain

What the weirdo can do for you...

Are you anxious to meet your weirdo within? It is very simple, really. All you need to do is find one thing you love more than anything else in the world and then do that thing. At first people will laugh at the weirdo and mock you for following its impulse. But after a month or two, when the initial fanfare has died down, those same people will gather from far and wide to admire the great things your weirdo has accomplished. They will praise you as a "visionary" or a "genius" and bestow upon you their exalted humdrum honors. They will celebrate your originality as "insightful" and regard your past weirdness as a "brilliant" step in the direction of your dreams.

The different sorts of madness are innumerable.
-Rabelais

I know it sounds strange, but this is how the humdrummers operate. They scoff at anything that is different until they have found some way to rationalize it in their humdrum minds. Don't be a victim of their evil snares. Expect it as a necessary step on the path to Crazy-Wisdom. Even find ways to look forward to it because it means you're in the Crazy-Master minority circle---and you're living your life apart from the humdrum crowd.

Mad, mad, everyone is
mad, So why are people
criticized for it?
When you dive into the
ocean of the heart, you see
that the only
madman is truly God.
-Baul Poet

5. THE INSANE GUIDE TO OUTRAGEOUSNESS...

What does the Crazy-Master really have to be afraid of? Is he afraid of rejection? Laughter? Scorn?

The Crazy-Master chuckles at these conditions. If people laugh at him what does he care? He's too busy laughing at himself to notice. If people mock and reject his way of life he hardly has time to take offense---he's having too much fun to even care.

For example, while a normal person might complain that the lines at the supermarket are too long or the service is not what it should be, the Crazy-Master might sing a Bay City Roller's ballad or juggle bags of potato chips or start a jelly bean fight. He will do anything except complain about how the world is. If someone grumbles to him about the weather or whines about a particular stock that isn't doing well, the Crazy-Master might pinch that person's nose and shout "honk!" or in an authoritative voice say, "It's exactly three thirty three!" and then walk away. You may think that any normal person would regard such behavior as childish and silly, but in my experience, it is better to appear a bit ridiculous for a short moment than to endure the endless monotony of an addicted complainer.

> *Madness is tonic and invigorating.*
> *It makes the sane more sane.*
> *The only ones who are unable to profit by it are the insane.*
> -Henry Miller

Where is your outrageousness?

Being abnormal gives you a lot of latitude for behavior. The longer you work on your abnormalities, the longer you'll be able to do the things most normal people wouldn't dream.

If an abnormality goes to a party, no one will be shocked to see him being the first one out on the dance floor or watching with amusement as he livens up the mood with silly string or ridiculous costumes. In fact, what most normal people find shocking in themselves---they almost *expect* from the outrageous abnormality.

As A PRACTICAL JOKE TO SCARE HIS FRIENDS, NATHAN RAN OFF A CLIFF, MAKING THEM THINK HE JUST RAN OFF A CLIFF.

No explanations are necessary...

The more abnormal you become, the less you'll have to explain yourself to other people. At first, they will demand an explanation for *everything* you do, but as time progresses, your Crazy-Master behavior will prove itself too outrageous to even bother confronting. They will have labeled you a "nut" and then you are free to go about your business.

Madness is part of all of us, all the time, and it comes and goes, waxes and wanes.
-Otto Friedrich

The business of the Crazy-Master

Once the Crazy-Master is free from the influence of other people's infectious critical opinions---he will be pleasantly surprised with the ease and fluidity with which his life effortlessly flows. He is no longer bound by the manipulative demands of the ignorant humdrummers because he is no longer susceptible to their stifling critiques. He is doing his own thing his own way and answering to no one but his Crazy-Master within.

When I first made the switch in my own life, it was as if a giant veil lifted off my imagination. I had finally mustered up the courage to say "Enough! I will not look to outside humdrummers for my own interior validation! What I do is good for me to do because it makes me happy to do it. It brings me peace and contentment and makes me a better person as a result. To hell with humdrum thoughts! I am a Crazy-minded-Master and I will not think like the humdrum masses!"

My entire life took a dramatic turn with that proclamation. People, ideas, and opportunities began to flow into my life like never before. I went from being a lukewarm Crazy-Critter to a Master beyond my wildest dreams. My fears and inhibitions began to magically melt away and I felt the fire of internal Madness propel me forth into exciting and unforeseen territories.

Can it be that they are mad themselves, since they call me mad?
-Plautus

This is not something that happened over night. The path to Crazy-Wisdom is long and sometimes arduous. It is a road taken by few and laughed at by many. Life in the Crazy-Master speed-way can be a lonely journey---and if you break

38

down along the way, don't expect help any time soon. That is why the gifts of Crazy-Wisdom are so great. There are too few people there to enjoy the massive abundance, too few people to believe in the wisdom of what at first glance seems unwise.

> *It may be that the great prophets who appeared to mankind as mad were in reality raving with impotent sanity.*
> -G.K. Chesterton

My own abnormal quest...

When I was in my junior year of college I wanted to host my own television show. Most people thought it was a crazy idea. I asked a few professors about the plausibility of such a scheme and they all laughed. "Who wants to watch a nineteen year old on TV? Stick to your studies son---there is no place for you on television."

I thanked my professors for their enthusiasm and unbridled support and tossing my school books into the trash, I decided to give it a shot. I called every station within a fifty mile radius of Boston and pitched my amazing idea. And just as my insightful professors had predicted, not one station was interested in giving me an audition. I spent two months collecting rejections. No one was even willing to meet me face to face. "What experience have you got?" asked one entry level knuckle head. "Not much," I said. "But I'm a fast learner and I have an amazing idea!" "Sorry pal," came the reply, "we're not interested."

Then one day my luck changed. I was flipping through a few stations on TV when I happened upon a public access channel from a local station outside of Boston. I called them, explained my idea and within the month I had my own show. Now, you're probably saying, "public access? Big deal, anyone can do that!" And you're right, anyone can do it, but not exactly the way I did it.

The more perfect the love, the greater the madness.
-Erasmus

The program was called "Today's Entrepreneur" and was dedicated to the exploration of new ideas and concepts for aspiring business mavericks. Not very original---but here's the catch: instead of dragging guests over for the half hour interview on the set, I got myself a crew to take the show on the road. I would go anywhere---executive suites, back rooms, office cubicles and even in a kitchen! Entrepreneurs loved the idea of having a camera crew come to their offices and suites. It created energy and excitement for everyone involved. No one cared about my age or inexperience. If I made a glitch (which happened quite often!) I just kept going.

After a few months, the show had expanded into five more demographic areas. It grew a bit more after that and then leveled off. Because of the public-access situation, the show never became a commercial success---and that was just fine with me. I did something most people thought was impossible to do and had fun doing it. I met presidents of corporations, inventors, and Crazy-Master entrepreneurs. I got to talk with fascinating people and learn about the crazy things that made them tick.

My madness, I thank the King of heaven for it.
-Ma-da-Cherda

The experience taught me the value of Crazy-Master persistence and outrageousness. There is always a way to do something if you really want to do it. It may not be what you originally intended, but that's part of life. Flexibility is the key to Crazy-Master durability. And if you want to last--- sometimes you've got to act fast.

What is madness? It means total absorption in something other than that which is generally accepted as reality. When someone is totally absorbed in something that is limited to his own perception, and (is not available to) the perception of others, he is called mad.

-Baul Poet

6. THE INSANE GUIDE TO THE MASTER PLAN OF MADNESS...

The Crazy-minded-Master has a master plan of madness---a dream or mystical vision that stirs his super-abundance of crazy energy and diligence into every creative endeavor he enacts. He knows the value of this impassioned insanity. He knows the power of unbridled enthusiasm and employs its energy into every dimension of his thought.

If the Crazy-Master has a dream to become a best selling author he does not wait until he writes a best selling book, but rather he becomes a best selling author the moment he decides to be so. He has no contacts? No book? No ideas? No money? No writing style? So what! His dream is too big to worry about details. Once the Crazy-Master realizes deep inside that a best selling author is who he *really* is, then all the details begin taking on a life of their own. Ideas suddenly begin to pour in. Contacts begin to mysteriously emerge. A writing style of his own begins to develop. His enthusiasm eventually begets every aspect of his dream. The world begins to align itself with what the Crazy-Master knew all along---and then suddenly---to the astonishment of everyone around---this master plan of madness is no longer as crazy as it once seemed.

"Mad" is a term we use to describe a man who is obsessed with one idea and nothing else.
-Ugo Betti

What is your master plan of madness?...

Can you think of something you want to do more than anything else in the world? A project or vocation that would keep you awake late every night and jolt you up early every morning? Some of you may not have any such vocation.

And my suggestion for you is the same suggestion I would give to any Crazy-Master: try lots of new things. On Tuesday learn to ride a unicycle, on Wednesday learn how to operate a back hoe, on Thursday learn how to juggle wet fish. Try one new thing every day for thirty days. I guarantee you will find *some thing, person or vocation* that will excite you within that time.

Go to the zoo and enlist.
Shave your neighbor's dog. Yo!
Dump your spaghetti on that
guy's head.
-Inside the ears of crazy people
-Gary Larson The Far Side

Where are your crazy intuitions leading you? What dreams would you pursue if you knew they were before you now? Would you drive across the country on a motorcycle? Would you start that novel you always wanted to write? How about learning to scuba dive or peddling your handmade jewelry to the local shops in your area? The Crazy-Master never concerns himself with *how* he is going to achieve his dreams, he is only attentive to the clarity of the dream itself. If he knows what he wants---in exquisite and exact detail---if his vision is all encompassing and complete, then the appropriate steps of attainment will reveal themselves accordingly.

It seems to me great wisdom
in a person if she wishes to go
mad for God.
-Iacopone da Todi

If he wants to paint beautiful pictures but has never had a lesson in his life---he may start out as a finger painter or maybe begin his career coloring by numbers. What the Crazy-Master will never do is to spend years pouring over books and going to lectures on painting without having ever touched a brush. The Crazy-Master motto is "Try something first, figure out how to do it later." If he wants to write music, he does not spend fifteen years learning how to play instruments before ever putting his musical ideas on paper. If he can't play anything then he'll buy a kazoo. If he can't play the kazoo then he'll whistle, if he can't whistle then he'll hum.

There is always a way! And if the technical expertise isn't there, then he'll make up for it with his expertise in insanity and *act as* if he is an expert!

Experts?

The humdrummers never do anything interesting because they are afraid of appearing incompetent. But what happens when we start observing our so-called "experts"? Are they competent at everything they do? Of course not! Do they make mistakes---even in the field of their expertise? You bet! That's what makes their lives so great. We are all brailing our way through what we do. No one ever becomes so adept at a job or skill that they have nothing new to learn. There is always something new! Even if you have the perfect hamburger flip, there is still room for improvement---still room to grow.

Humdrummers never really get this point. They seldom plan anything because they don't know how to be competent at incompetence. They have to be the expert tennis player *before* they take their lessons or else they will never touch a racket. This kind of thinking is absolutely piddley! Half the fun of playing tennis is *learning how* to play. Watching as your backhand improves, learning the fundamentals of movement and anticipating your opponents technique. This isn't just learning how to play tennis this is learning how to play life! The expert tennis player is much like the expert Crazy-Master. He is always open to new improvements and techniques. He is never too advanced to step back into the beginners circle and never too proud to be humbled by a little beginner's humiliation.

Being crazy and doing crazy things is what keeps me sane.
-Debbie Shenefield

7. THE INSANE GUIDE TO BRAIN-DEAD PENCIL PUSHERS...

When hiring someone for an important project or for a position in a company, the Crazy-Master never looks for the brain-dead pencil pushers to fill in the vital roles in the organization---but rather he looks for the mono-maniacs intoxicated with the spirit of unencumbered insanity.

Any shlump can do a good job. It takes no imagination to do what you're hired to do on paper. That's why the Crazy-Master looks for the man or woman with an imaginative mission.

Missions are bigger than any single individual and require great outputs of creative flair to successfully accomplish. If the Crazy-Master is to utilize his amazing imaginative powers he must first acknowledge the potential madness such imagination may engender.

I have defined the 100% American as 99% an idiot. And they just adore me.

-George Bernard Shaw

The morality of madness...

The Crazy-Master is never crazy for the sake of being crazy. His madness is an insanity with a higher purpose. Adolph Hitler was a crazy man---but he had no benevolent mission. A Crazy-Master is crazy for the benefit of life and the world in which he finds himself. Hitler's purpose was one of self-destruction and hatred. He had no spiritual connection to his mad behavior and as a result he was killed by the very unspiritual insanity for which he stood.

What separates the Crazy-Master from the loony humdrum sociopath? It is his realization of the inter-connectedness of all existence. He senses the patterns of goodness and truth in his behavior that elude even the most astute, perceptive humdrum loony-loon. The Crazy-Master chooses his madness for vitality and energetic delight. He feels the movement of God in his madness and acts in accordance with that perception. There is nothing crazy about his

50

insanity! It is direct and focused with the intention of creating happiness, passion and joy.

If only men would be mad in the same fashion and comfortably, they might manage to agree fairly well together.
-Bacon

Where is your mission of madness?

Do you want the unique ability to do what you want when you want to do it? Do you want to live an authentic, creative life full of autonomy, imagination and head spinning freedom? Then you must have the courage to do what you're afraid to do.

What are you afraid of? Are you afraid of meeting new people? Does your heart cringe whenever you're introduced to someone you've never met? If so, then you have a lot of fun things you can do to make up for it.

First off, you must absolutely understand that every person on this planet has the same fear. It is not an easy thing to introduce ourselves to new people. The fear of rejection is always a possibility and therefore a serious factor for the humdrum way of life. But as Crazy-Masters we have a few interesting ways to deal with that fear.

Sanity is madness put to good use.
-George Santayana

The Crazy-Master fear-buster...

I first learned about the fear-buster when I was thirteen years old. I was desperately afraid of meeting new people (especially girls) and did everything in my power to avoid such situations. I'll never forget the day when a wise, old friend named Charles pulled me aside and gave me a few interesting suggestions,

"You know why you're so afraid of meeting new people?"

"No," I said, "why?"

"You are afraid of meeting new people because you haven't learned about the fear-buster!"

"What's the fear-buster?" I asked.

"It's an ancient fear killing technique---one afternoon of fear-busting, and you'll never be afraid again!"

Common sense, know-how---gone. So they say I'm crazy. Let them. All I ask, my crazy God, is that you stay put.
-Ramprasad

Charles took me to a local shopping center and said, "now look, you're gonna tip-toe yourself right into the grave until you learn to get a handle on what you're afraid of. Now I'm gonna show you something and I want you to follow my lead. Got it?"

"Got it." I said.

He then went up to the first person he saw (an attractive young woman) and said, "Hello, my name is Charles. I'm afraid of meeting new people so I'm trying to overcome that fear by speaking with you now."

I remember standing there humiliated and shocked. I was blushing brightly and had no idea what to do or say. Suddenly Charles pointed in my direction saying, "this is my good pal Lenny. He's also very scared of meeting you."

I looked up at Charles angrily. I was embarrassed that he had put me in such an awkward situation. "I am not afraid!" I said

53

stepping forward, pushing Charles out of the way and shouted, "HELLO, my name is LENNY. PLEEEASED to meet you!"

The young woman looked at us both like we were a couple of nuts and walked away. Charles and I looked at one another and broke out into hysterical laughter.

"Now comes step two Lenny. You have to do what I just did, only you have to do it fifty more times---and *then* you have to do it another hundred and fifty! I *guarantee* you'll never be afraid of meeting new people again."

"Two hundred times?" I asked.

"Two hundred." He said.

I felt a little ridiculous at first, but by person number eleven it was a piece of cake. In fact, after a while it became sort of a game and I actually began to enjoy myself.

*If a sane dog fights
a mad dog, it's the sane dog's
ear that is bitten off.*
-*Burmese Proverb*

"Hello!" I said to young woman number twenty -five, "my name is Lenny!"

"So what?" came the reply.

"So what? So what? So lets dance!"

I took hold of her left hand and her waist and began leading her around a department store like a complete idiot. There was no music playing so I made up my own.

"You're out of your mind!" she said.

"Maybe I am---but it got me to meet you!"

She was not impressed with my corn-ball one liner, but it got her attention. And incidentally, the more absurd I became with my ridiculous behavior, the easier it was for me to be comfortable just being myself. I figured if I could act like a complete idiot and not *feel* like an idiot, then I would never have to be afraid of occasionally acting like an idiot when I was trying to be myself!

Perhaps life itself seems lunatic, who knows where madness lies? Perhaps to be too practical is madness. To seek treasure where there is trash. Too much sanity may be madness.
-The Man of LaMancha

55

I think I got up to two twenty-three when Charles said I had fear-busted the hell out of my apprehension. He said that I had graduated with honors and will never have to be afraid of meeting new people again.

I've really never been afraid of meeting anyone since. Once in a while my stomach will turn a bit when I meet someone "important", but then I just remember how good it feels to be a Crazy-Master-idiot in the face of difficult situations---and the fear naturally goes away. It is amazingly liberating when the big frightening things in life become the very things that give us the biggest laugh---because after all, if we never learn to laugh at the pain, we'll never learn to live through the pleasure.

There is a pleasure sure
in being mad which none
but madmen know.
-Dryden

8. THE INSANE GUIDE TO PETTY GAB...

The Crazy-Master is an expert at developing and expressing opinions that directly contradict the status quo. If ever he finds himself trapped in some ridiculous conversation about the weather or his neighbor's shoe size, instead of becoming impatient or rude, the Crazy-Master has some fun with the situation.

For example, if someone says, "It's supposed to be a nice day tomorrow!"

He might say, "no it isn't, they're expecting a blizzard."

"But it's the middle of July!"

"I know, isn't that strange?" and then he'll walk away and let the glib-gabber try to figure it out.

The point of the contradictions is not to sound belligerent or rude (or even necessarily coherent) but instead, they are little reminders about the poisonousness of uninspired, petty gab. And while they may not change anyone's conversational habits---at least gabbers will think twice before talking to a Crazy-minded-Master.

Some accidents happen in life from which we have need of a little madness to extricate ourselves successfully.
-Rochefoucauld

Contradicting the status quo...

Spend a good part of each day baffling the promoters of petty gab. If one of them says to you "Boy, life's a real drag." say to him, "no it's not, it's a chicken." If he then asks, "How can life be a chicken?" say, "Exactly!" and then walk away.

If someone says, "I'm soooo tired of my job..." say, "no you're not, you love your job. It's all those damn turtles that wear you out!"

"Turtles? What are you talking about?"

Pretend to be a bit agitated and say, "YOU KNOW EXACTLY WHAT I'M TALKING ABOUT!!" And then walk away.

The purpose of these ridiculous responses is to force the petty gabber to actually *listen* to what is being said in any given conversation. The problem of petty gab is not what gabbers are *saying* but what they are *not hearing*.

Most petty gabbers gab because they are too lazy to listen. When you say nonsensical things in response to their gab, it shocks them out of the gab-induced sleep and forces them to pay attention to the conversation.

If someone nonchalantly says to you, "How's it going pal?" Instead of letting such a golden opportunity go with a drab, conventional response like, "not bad, thanks for asking!"--- Try this fun experiment instead: Stop immediately in your tracks, stare pointedly into the questioner's eyes, and say, "Ya know Harry I'm glad you asked!" And then go into an amazingly detailed account of your aunt Thelma's bout with rectal cancer or your uncle Ted's urinary tract infection. The point is to make the petty gabber think twice about asking you something he really doesn't give two shakes about. Watch how he shifts nervously from foot to foot. He may even look at his watch or remind you of some appointment he has in two minutes. But don't let him off so easy! The more impatient he becomes---the more you have to slow down in your descriptions. Teach this bugger a lesson---that all his inquiries have repercussions! And if he chooses to ask careless questions then he must be willing to pay the price and hear your very carefully scripted answers.

Petty gab can be fun humdrum to deal with because most petty gabbers are either too weak or too afraid to really call you on your tricks. They will go along with the game until you choose to end it---and for God's sake don't end it any time soon---make em' squirm!

Teach me half the gladness
That thy brain must know,
Such harmonious madness
From my lips would flow,
The world should listen then,
as I am listening now.
-Percy Bysshe Shelley

9. THE INSANE GUIDE TO REASONS...EXPLANATIONS...AND RATIONAL JUSTIFICATIONS...

There is no use asking the Crazy-Master why he is the way he is. Explanations as to why he behaves and thinks the way he does is a bit like trying to explain why a dog wags his tail one way and not another. Crazy-Master behavior cannot be explained because no explanation can possibly do it justice. Crazy-Masters do what Crazy-Masters do precisely because it is what they decide to do. Justifications and rationalizations are left for the humdrum buggers to try and widdle out between their own meddlesome neurosis's.

Humdrummers have necessary explanations for everything they do. If they are working at a job they hate, they will have a whole list of reasons why they have to remain faithful to their unhappily-chosen vocation. If they are married to a miserable partner, they will be able to justify the commitment with long winded appeals to duty, honor, and other emotional incarcerations supposedly owed to the spouse.

Humdrummers live dull, meaningless lives because they have "reasonable" explanations for every dull choice they make. Their decisions are logical, justifiable and follow a fairly predictable pattern. They have lives that "make sense" to their dim uninterested minds and are deemed "acceptable" to the dim uninterested people with whom they associate.

There are no explanations...

Try this little experiment the next time someone asks you a question about why you do what you do. If someone says to you, "Why do you spend so much time eating chocolate cake?" say, "because I want to!" If someone asks you, "Why do you read so many books?" or "Why do you want to quit school and travel the world?" or "Why are you acting so strangely?" say coolly and unemotionally, "because I want to!"

This response, as simple as it appears, is a declaration of your unreasonable independence. It is your ticket to your emotional freedom from the manipulative rationalizations of other humdrum rascals.

> *Tact consists in knowing how*
> *far to go too far.*
> -Jean Cocteau

Most humdrummers seek reasonable explanations for the Crazy-Master's peculiar eccentricities because they want to trap him into an endless array of logical justifications and amendments for what he chooses to do. Don't get caught in their trap! You have no reason to explain anything to anyone. You are the Crazy-Master of your own life. The Crazy-Creator of your own destiny. If you want to jog through the Himalayas on your seventieth birthday---you have nothing to explain. If what you do makes your world a better, more joyful place, then that is all the justification you need.

You have one Crazy-Master life to live so live it! Don't explain it, feel it! Don't justify it, experience it! If things don't always make sense to the humdrum crowd---too bad! Your attempt to rationalize and explain won't make sense to them anyway. You operate from a different point of reference, a more powerful space of realization. Get used to this tension. You will be misunderstood by most people most of your life, and as the Crazy-Creator of your own experience, such misunderstandings are a welcomed delight.

I owe my success to having listened respectfully to the very best advice, and then going away and doing the exact opposite.
-G.K. Chesterton

10. THE INSANE GUIDE TO BORE-DUMB...

The Crazy-Master faces every monotonous situation as an opportunity for his jolly madness. If he is trapped in a dull lecture you won't find him gazing numbly at the speaker with half shut eyes and a tranquilized brain---instead he might be drawing caricatures of some of the people in the audience or perhaps learning a new trick like sticking a pencil up his nose.

The Crazy-Master is never bored because he is never boring. His life is often a very entertaining spectacle to behold. Full of enchanting inconsistencies and amusing occasions of utterly inspired folly.

For example, if it is commonly expected that a person should wait politely (numbly) in line at the local bank or post office, the Crazy-Master might take to singing some silly song at the top of his lungs or bring in two dozen doughnuts and hand them out to the people in line. If he is stuck still in a traffic jam, instead of whining and whimpering about whatever nonsense comes to mind, the Crazy-Master might wave to all the other cars like he's at an Easter parade or sit on top of his car roof and get a sun tan.

> *Boredom is the feeling that everything is a waste of time; serenity, that nothing is.*
> -Thomas Szasz

Bore-dumb is meaningless to the Crazy-Master because he is always aware of so many other alternatives. There is nothing ever worth complaining about. If it rains the Crazy-Master jumps through puddles. If it's a bad month at the office, he simply tightens his belt and eats grass for a while. There is always another option. Always! There are no dull situations there are only dull, unimaginative responses.

And for the Crazy-Master, such responses are a fate worse than death.

In a sane world madness is the only freedom!
  -J.   Ballarde

What are your alternatives?

How do you respond to dull circumstances? Do you accept bore-dumb as a necessary part of your existence?   Are blunted, boring people attracted to you because you accept and affirm their monotony?   Do you affirm the monotony in your own life?

Zorba: *You've got everything...except one thing; madness...a man needs a little madness or else...*

Boss: *Or else?*

Zorba: *He never dares cut the rope and be free.*
  -Nikos Kazantzakis

The dullest man in the world...

The most amazing specimen of dullness is not tedium we experience at the podium but the dullness we experience in our minds. When confronted with a boring situation, it is not the situation that bores us but our unimaginative responses to such situations.

I once knew a man that worked in the busiest hospital in the South Bronx. Every day was filled with new adventures, hundreds of people coming and going. Gun shot wounds, battered victims of muggings, hit and run accidents, and drug overdoses were almost a daily occurrence. There were ten times more hospitalized people than there were hospital staff to treat them. The situation was an endless array of frantic activity and movement, a hodgepodge of medicine, madness and your occasional miracle.

What intrigued me most about this hospital was a man who worked as an orderly, I'll call him Patrick. Patrick was the laziest man I've ever seen. No matter how fast things moved around him---he would still trudge along at his same lethargic pace. People in every corner were in desperate need of attention, love and care---but poor lazy Pat moved as though he were rolling over in his sleep.

Life is half insanity as we choose to make it.

-George Margretson

I had an occasion to talk with Patrick during a church picnic at the parish I was visiting. He mentioned to me that he'd been working at the hospital for over eleven years when I said to him, "Boy, working at a hospital in the Bronx must be exciting!"

Patrick: "Actually it is a rather dull place to work."

Len: "Dull? There must be a million adventures every night! I bet you've got some stories to tell!"

Patrick: "Stories? Not me. I'm just an orderly---not too much happens in my job."

Well it wasn't until about two weeks later when I had to take a friend into the South Bronx Hospital that I had the occasion to witness lazy Pat's lethargy first hand. I found the entire spectacle amazing! There Patrick was---in one of the most stimulating places in all of New York and he could barely stop looking at his watch. Millions of adventures right in front of his face and he can hardly keep his eyes open wide enough to see them!

DEFINITIVE PROOF FOR SURVIVAL OF THE LEAST FIT.

A remedy for dullness...

The best thing to do if you are bored is realize that you are not bored you are boring. You must remove the blame from an outside source (i.e. a boring speaker or a boring class) and transform your experience of "blaming" into self-examination and introspective responsibility for how and what you feel.

Though I am mad, I will not bite him.
-Shakespeare
Antony and Cleopatra

The Crazy-Master never gets bored. In fact he doesn't even know how! If he is confronted with a situation that *appears* to be dull---he always finds a way to liven things up.

Life is only dull for dull people---and for the Crazy-Master no tedious situation is beyond his ability to incorporate his exhilarating methods of devious rascality. Look for these characters the next time you're stuck at a dull, monotonous event. Or better yet, become one yourself and watch how the sparks start to fly!

> *My act is about how you have to be completely crazy to survive.*
> -Steve Martin

11. THE INSANE GUIDE TO YOUR CRAZY-MASTER EDUCATION...

Humdrummers like to get into the newspapers. They like award banquets and pompous ceremonies that trumpet their mediocrity. They often have many trophies and plaques cluttering their living areas and offices and join clubs and organizations for the many nifty "certificates of achievement" they can hang on their walls.

They are also very taken with titles, degrees and funny little letters after their names. They enjoy reiterating past feats and accomplishments and spend ample amounts of time telling people how much time they've spent in schools and universities to become the educated humdrummers that they are.

Humdrummers love applause. They can't get enough of it. If they are doing something ridiculous and people clap, they will continue doing it until the clapping stops. They are somewhat like a trained poodle being rewarded with a pat on the head every time he pees on the neighbor's shrubbery. They have no idea about the consequences of their mindless behavior, they just can't live a day without the sleep inducing accolade.

The Crazy-Master cannot stand the applause. For him, notoriety means nothing more than mediocre recognition for something he would have done anyway. He lives his life the way he wants---whether anyone knows about it or not. People can laugh or applaud and it will all be the same to him. If he does something silly and the world approves of his behavior---it makes no difference to him. And if he does something magnificent and the world abhors his behavior, so much the better!

The Crazy-Master needs nothing of the world's attention. He prefers the anonymity of the "unknown" masses but knows his Crazy-Master behavior makes him a unique spectacle for all the world to see.

> ## *I guess the definition of a lunatic is a man surrounded by them.*
> -Ezra Pound

The educated moron...

Why do we do the things we do? Do we do them because it is what makes sense deep inside or do we do them because someone else approves? Are you going to school because it is the accepted thing or are you really interested in an education? Are you joining the "Ivy League" universities because you truly believe you can get superior training in your chosen field, or are you more concerned with the reputation and stature of the school?

What is an education? Is it a fancy degree hanging on a wall or is it something much more profound? That depends on who you ask. A humdrummer might walk into the office of an idiot, and seeing all the magnificent university paraphernalia on the wall, assume that the idiot is really quite intelligent. In fact, he may put his financial destiny in the hands of such a moron and allow him to handle his entire investment portfolio. You may laugh---but I've seen it happen!

There are many educated morons sitting behind very large desks, smoking fancy cigars, and repeating very elaborate lines from Shakespeare and Chaucer. Many educated morons are extremely well read. They have all kinds of intricate theories about nothing in particular and follow current events like they were to be tested on them the next day.

The Crazy-Master education...

What is an education? Aren't the educated men or women the ones who live life freely, without the mindless worries and concerns of the humdrum masses? The purpose of a Crazy-

Master education is one that leads to happiness, creativity, and joy.

Sometimes a scream is better than a thesis.

-Emerson

How does our contemporary educational system add up? Does it lead our students to Crazy-Master freedom or is it training them for the humdrum masses? The answer to that question lies in the student body such institutions attract. For instance, if a young person is interested in becoming abnormally unique in this world, if he or she wants to design a life independently of the humdrum herd, how can our contemporary institutions respond to so great a challenge? Is it even possible for a budding Crazy-Master to find nurture and support in so stifling an environment?

We must first investigate the purpose of our higher educational environments. Why do they exist? And more importantly, why have we assumed such enormous importance to every man, woman, and child passing through their gates? Is a university the only real place one can find an education? Are their environments really conducive to creative, explorative thought?

It depends upon what one considers an education. If an education is reading fine books, attending interesting lectures, and passing examinations, then most of our institutions are doing their jobs, they are educating their students. If however, an education is the facilitation of imaginative and creative thinking then most of our institutions are hopelessly lost. Our contemporary institutions do not encourage creative, intuitive thinking. They not only do not, they can not. They are not designed for creative and imaginative stimulation, they are designed to critique and assimilate ideas that have already been created and imagined. New ideas from students are generally not welcomed in the university setting. They are invited but not welcomed. And as a result we are not educating our students to think but educating them to be educated.

> *God created man because he was so disappointed in the monkey.*
> -Mark Twain

The Crazy-Master University...

Imagine a university that acknowledges the full spectrum of human intelligence. Imagine a place where emotional as well as intellectual explorations are encouraged. And the power of creativity and imagination is as widely espoused as the powers of dissection and conceptualization. Imagine the possibilities of such a university? Imagine the power it would bestow upon all those that attend?

Life is trouble. Only death is not!
To be alive is to undo your belt
and look for trouble!
-Zorba the Greek

It is my belief that this grass roots Crazy-Master movement will demand such holistic educational services. I am certain that the more you develop into your Crazy-Master power the more you will demand such excellence in education.

After all, what Crazy-Master wants to get a humdrum education? Who wants to learn the same things everyone else is learning? And unless your field is something specific like law or medicine, there is absolutely no reason whatsoever that humiliating regurgitative exams and tests need be part of the system. Who needs exams? All they do is cause sleepless nights and unwanted busy-work. Why not learn how to love the subject matter instead of being forced to assimilate it against your will? Contemporary examinations are designed primarily to measure one's convergent "problem solving" intelligence while ignoring the entire spectrum of divergent "creative and formulative" intelligence. Most Crazy-Masters have an immense inventive and imaginative capacity that cannot be adequately measured with our ordinary, unimaginative standardized examinations. In fact, if intelligence were the colors of a rainbow, most scholastic aptitude tests would be stuck measuring three different shades of brown!

Our system of grading is closely tied in with this nonsense. Why do we need grades? When I was in college, I noticed how agitated and nervous these little letters made me feel. Whenever I saw an "A" I felt elated, whenever I saw a "C" or a "D", I felt depressed and miserable. I remember during my sophomore year telling myself, "I don't need this! Enough!" And I vowed never to look at my grades again. It was one of the most liberating experiences I'd ever had. While my peers were sweating and fretting over their class rank and busy "making nice" with all their teachers---I was free. I studied material because I wanted to learn it. Nothing more. If I didn't like a class, I would tell the teacher. I wasn't afraid of what he or she might do to me because there was nothing he or she could do. Could my grade be lowered? If it was, I never knew about it. I never looked at my test scores or report cards. Other students thought I was nuts, but who's kidding who? I didn't care about my academic record in some vault in the school administrative building---I cared only about the education that I was paying good money to receive.

Why not whip the teacher when the student misbehaves?
-Diogenes

Also, why force students to attend classes? If the subject matter and professor are really worth their exorbitant fee (most university classes cost $40 per hour!) then the classes should be interesting enough to warrant so high a price. When I pay six bucks to see a movie---I expect my six bucks worth! If it's a terrible movie, I'll ask for my money back. Imagine interrupting a university professor mid way through a boring class and demand that you get your money back? Not a bad idea for your own Crazy-Master education!

Some solutions...

There are no institutional changes that can compare to the interior changes one must develop as a Crazy-Master. We can analyze and discuss the various challenges we face as Crazy-Master disciples---but the real solutions will emerge once we begin looking at our own lives and the influence our Crazy-minded-thinking can have on our own immediate surroundings.

I challenge you not so much to challenge the system, but I challenge you to challenge yourself. There is no greater power than the power gotten from your own interior motives. Don't get too critical or too angry at the way things look right now. Such negative emotions work too much against your Crazy-Master way of life. Be content and walk humbly. Your work begins with yourself and your education begins with your reaction to everything else. Don't let the world get you down. It is the way it is. And irrespective of any opinion to the contrary---it's exactly what its supposed to be.

To define true madness,
what is't but to be nothing else
but mad?
-Shakespeare

12. THE INSANE GUIDE TO TELEVISION PLANTERS...

The Crazy-Master never reads commercial newspapers or magazines. If he owns a television it is used only as a shelf to keep potted plants or perhaps a place to put an ice cold beer on a hot summer day.

The Crazy-Master has no room for the mass media in his life. He has nothing against it per se, he just prefers to live his life simply, enjoying the simple pleasures of reading good books and discussing topical issues with close friends.

If the Crazy-Master engages any kind of visual media it will be in the form of unusual movies and well planned documentaries. Such creations stimulate his crazy-creative powers and often propel his thoughts into wild uncharted territory.

Insanity destroys reason but not wit.
-Emmons

Where is your creative madness?

Do you want to be more creative? Do you want to propel your imagination into new and uncharted territory? Then you must become your own entertainment. Game shows and television sitcoms are imaginative poison. They rob of us of our ingenuity and chatter the brain into passive monotony.

For example, if 90% of your laughter comes from commercial entertainers and comedians, do you think you will exert the necessary effort to discover what is comical and humorous in your own life? Most people have great difficulty making themselves laugh. They need outside stimulation in order to appreciate the more waggish aspects of their existence. They need someone else to tell them what's funny and what's appropriate for merriment.

Don't be a passive comedian! Find your own interior clown and let it loose. Life is an amazingly funny place. There are a thousand and one things to laugh about in any given moment, if only you take the moment to notice them.

*He was born with the gift of
laughter and a sense that the
world was mad.*
-Raphael Sabatini

Funny things to do today...

Do you need some humor in your life? Go to the Post Office and watch all the humdrum people anxiously awaiting their turns. Watch how some get angry at the silliest little things and grumble about the price of stamps or the lethargy of some of the workers. Or go to the Registry of Motor Vehicles and watch some of the sour faced employees move around like their arms are weighed down with ten tons of wet lettuce. My favorite past time is to go to department stores two or three days before Christmas. I usually come home with a half dozen amusing anecdotes from a simple half hour visit!

*It is by not confining one's
neighbors that one is convinced
of one's own sanity.*
-Dostoevsky

13. THE INSANE GUIDE TO NICETIES...

The Crazy-Master is not concerned with appropriate social customs and rules. In fact, he is very much amused with the absurd lengths most people go to in order to make such a favorable social impression.

Kissing hands, bowing at the waist, pretend smiles, forced phony chortles and chuckles, ridiculous one liners, nonsensical inquiries into things one cares nothing about, deceptive nods of interest and attention---the list goes on. The Crazy-Master is sickened by such charades. If he doesn't want to talk to a particular person, he does not make up phony excuses or pretend to see someone vying for his attention across the room, rather he simply and sincerely informs the person of his desire to be *un-engaged*---and, without guile or guilt, walks away from the conversation.

The normal humdrummer may find such behavior reprehensible but is it any less reprehensible to deceptively *pretend* to be interested in a bore? Is the truth not one thousand times more refreshing? So simple. So direct. No phony exterior. No conflicting messages or facades. What could be more desirable in human interaction?

TWO NICE GUYS IN HELL

When do you "make nice"?

When someone puts a hand out to you do you automatically take it? Most people do. In fact, most everyone will find you quite rude if you don't. Why is this? Have we become so ingrained with societal "expectations" that this is the extent of our imaginative possibilities?

How about when someone sneezes? Do you always say "God bless you" Why not say it when people burp? Or perhaps when they hic-up? Or what about kissing someone when you say hello. Have you ever thought of licking them instead? Dogs do this and always get a favorable response.

(Incidentally, the phrase "God bless you" originated in 1648 with the Black Plague. If a person sneezed during the plague, that person was likely to die within a few days. It is the Dark Ages' equivalent to saying, "Kiss your ass good-bye!")

I have a friend who shakes people's hands with his thumb held down. When the other person notices the strange sensation of shaking a thumbless hand, my friend nonchalantly whispers, "I sometimes forget to put my thumb up!" He usually gets an initial stare of bewilderment followed by either chagrin or laughter. Another thing he frequently does is to reach for a woman's hand and bringing it up to his lips---he kisses his own! He tells her, "you can't be too careful these days!"

The point is not to embarrass people into uncomfortable situations but to subtly and quietly be the reminder of Crazy-

Wisdom in this sanely de-spired, dull little world. The Crazy-Master imposes every social engagement with his candor and truth. Whether he is speaking to a drunk on the street or a King in a castle he uses the same straight-shooting crazy conversational style. He is not impressed with stature and position, he is impressed only with the Crazy-Wisdom of a social misfit gone mad!

What is madness
To those who only observe,
is often wisdom
To those whom it happens.
-Christopher Fry

14. THE INSANE GUIDE TO PIDDLEY OPINIONS...

The Crazy-Master expresses no opinions to the outside world. And as strange and unconventional as this disposition may initially seem---it becomes rather refreshing to anyone engaged in a Crazy-Master conversation. For instance, ask any culturally fit misfit on the street what he thinks about international diplomacy tactics between Iran and the population of the planet Pluto---and he will eagerly respond with a list of things he has heard or read someplace in his limited and thoughtless travels. Ask him if what he is saying is true and he will usually respond with a resounding, "Yes! Of course it's true!" He will have no foundational reference for such opinions because he has no idea why or how he has come to such beliefs.

Most humdrummers don't read books or travel anywhere outside their immediate area and often refer to the evidence of "they say..." for scientific proof of their convictions. They do not inquire deeply into things and they are satisfied with the surface sound bites from their local news-casters and tabloid papers.

If you ask the Crazy-Master for his opinions he will rarely respond with a coherent series of convictions. Most humdrummers regard such incoherence as ignorance or feeble-mindedness but in truth, his worst rambling incoherence is more coherent than the humdrummer's best coherent analysis of what opinions he is currently defending as truth.

The man pulling radishes
pointed the way with
a radish.
-Issa

Where are your piddley opinions?

Try this experiment next time someone asks you for your opinion about a particular politician or the weather or some sport celebrity. If someone asks you, "What's your opinion about candidate X" or "What's the weather supposed to be for next week?" say firmly and without emotion, *"I don't know."*

Even if you do know the answer practice keeping your opinions to yourself. This little exercise does two things for your Crazy-Master within. First, it shows you how useless most opinions are to most people. Humdrummers don't really care about what you have to say about politics or the weather. They use their "interest" in your opinions as a springboard to telling you their own.

Forgive me my nonsense as I also forgive the nonsense of those who think they talk sense.
-Robert Frost

You will soon grow accustomed to the idea that most humdrummers don't even notice or care that you have nothing to say and jump right in where you left off with all the energy and enthusiasm of a second rate game show host. Also, you will become regarded as a person of great knowledge and wisdom because you participate so little during piddley conversations. I don't know why this is, but humdrummers find the quietest people the most intelligent during social interactions.

It is now clear to me that there is no difference between ourselves and the people in a madhouse; at the time I only vaguely suspected this, and like all madmen, I thought everyone except myself was mad.

-Leo Tolstoy
On his status as a well-respected literary professor

Humdrummers are so busy arranging and explaining their own ideas that they wouldn't have any room for your opinions anyway. It is a relief for them to speak without obstruction and disagreements and they will reward your patience with their endless prattle about this or that. Look to this experiment as your Crazy-Master social training. It is best to keep your mouth silent and the world guessing. Your Crazy-Master life will keep them guessing nonetheless---so why not let them guess a little more?

The world calls me mad.
I am mad, you are mad,
all the world is mad. Who
in the world is not mad?
Still they call me mad.
Some are mad after name
and fame. Some are mad
after money. Some are
mad after skin. But blessed
is he who is mad after God.
I am a madcap of that
type.
-Sri Rang Avadhoot

15. THE INSANE GUIDE TO NORMAL PEOPLE...

Most "normal" people look at a Crazy-Master as a bizarre deviation from the acceptable standard. They see his zany, unpretentious behavior as somewhat mysterious; an oddity apart from their "accepted" perceptions of their life and their reality.

For example, when a normal person looks at the world he sees everything that's gone wrong with it. He is looking at a beautiful sunrise and instead of admiring the subtle shades of red and orange, he will complain about having had to get up so early. If he is dining at a fine restaurant he will complain that his broccoli is too green or that he is seated too close to the kitchen or that the napkins are a ghastly match to the table clothe. Nothing seems to please the "normal" humdrummer because he is obviously so displeased with himself.

Explore what you are scoffed at for wanting to explore.
-Crazy-Master Maxim

The Crazy-Master perceives the world in an exact opposite way. If his car breaks down on the highway he does not kick the tires and scream and carry on like a small child that just spilled ice cream, but rather the Crazy-Master uses the opportunity to get some exercise jogging to the nearest gas station or he tries to fix the problem himself or he juggles stones from the side of the road until help arrives. In other words, the Crazy-Master pro-actively pursues creative solutions rather that endlessly focusing on the obviousness of the problem. He finds opportunities where "normal" people find strife and frustration. It is the difference between insanity and Crazy-Creativity---the difference between of the Crazy-Master and the slow, putrid, decay of a "normal" person's experience.

> *Slipping into madness*
> *is good for the sake of*
> *comparison.*
> -Jenny Holzer

Normal abnormalities...

Are you too normal? Do you seem to fit in everywhere you go like a pair of comfortable pants?

The Crazy-Master is like a strip of bright yellow wallpaper. He can't seem to make himself fit in anywhere. If he's at a somber wake, he'll be the one in the back telling amusing stories about the deceased.   If he's at a tea party, he might be drinking scotch instead. If he's at a bar, he might be the only one in the place drinking a chocolate malt.

There is something refreshing about the Crazy-Masters abnormality. It helps us see the abnormality in ourselves with a sense of lightness and joy. His madness makes everyone else want to be a little crazy for themselves.

*Great wits are to madness
near allied, and thin partitions
do their bounds divide.*
-John Dryden

One way not to be normal...

Whenever you go to a swimming pool or beach, always be the first one to jump in the water. Even if its a bit chilly, jump in right away. What have you got to lose? Don't be like the humdrummers who dip their toes and shiver on the side for twenty minutes before going in.

This behavior teaches your brain the power of immediate abnormal action. The people who stand on the sidelines of life experience more heartache from *inaction* than the Crazy-Master will ever experience from doing things immediately. "But what if the water's cold?" asks the humdrummer. Then I say jump in even quicker! The longer you ruminate about the possible discomfort of a potential situation, the more it will agonize you *before* you even try it!

What's the worst part about anything fearful? When I went skydiving, I was amazed at how much easier it became once I jumped out of the plane! The worst part was *thinking* about the jump. Once I was in the air it was a piece of cake. There was no time to be afraid because I had too many other things to concentrate on. I was too *busy* to be afraid. I was only afraid *before* the jump, when my brain had plenty of time to stir around the various fearful scenarios.

So I say jump now and think later. Always be the first one in. Let all the humdrummers shiver and shake on the sidelines. You're too busy having fun to worry about how cold it is once you're in!

The usefulness of a madman is famous: he demonstrates society's logic flagrantly carried down to its last scrimshaw scrap.
-Cynthia Ozick

16. THE INSANE GUIDE TO TALKING GIBBERISH...

When people approach the Crazy-Master and begin talking gibberish he has no other recourse than to talk gibberish right back.

If someone says to the Crazy-Master, "You won't believe what juicy gossip I just heard! Mrs. Enkelhauser told me that Betty Boobwinkel is cheating on her husband!"

The Crazy-Master's response might be something like, "Ik-alabob-bob-alaboo---you're a little orange chickaladee like a blue-bird in the zoo."

Of course, what he is saying makes absolutely no sense whatsoever---but what other response can possibly make sense to the ridiculous gossipy verbiage that makes no sense itself? If someone starts rambling on about nothing, does it serve any charitable purpose to engage that person in such inane, pathetic behavior?

If seeking the truth is the Crazy-Master's top priority, then *speaking* the truth is where he must logically begin. He must never lend an ear to such poisonous infected babble. Truth begins with actions and our actions begin with words--- the words the Crazy-Master speaks to himself.

If the Crazy-Master lives one way and then speaks another, such interior contradictions will eventually lead to his own destruction. He follows where his madness leads but never employs the misdirected madness of another person's jostled gibberish.

How do you respond to gibberish?

Do you accept the evil throes of mindless gossip? Are you quick to join the into hapless back stabbing harangue about another person's affairs? The Crazy-Master will never engage in such petty behavior. In fact, if a person wants to become a Crazy-Master then he must first and foremost learn the art of minding his own business.

This is a very difficult thing for humdrum people to get. They have such great interest in everyone else's lives because there is nothing going on in their own. They love talking about other people because they know no one is interested in talking about them.

Humdrum people are very lifeless and dull. They are like pieces of gum that get stuck to your shoe. You hardly notice them until you have somewhere important to go---and then--- lo and behold, there they are---holding you back with whatever strength their pathetic lives can muster.

We want a few mad people now. See where the sane ones have landed us!
-George Bernard Shaw

17. THE INSANE GUIDE TO YAK-YAK...

Yak-Yak is unlike gibberish because it incurs no hurtful or pernicious repercussions. It is petty gab taken to an absurd extreme: it is talking not for the sake of talking but for the sake of wasting time. It is somewhat like dumping a mug of water into the ocean, it makes a little noise at first but adds no real value to its overall dimension.

Yak-Yak is uninformed chatter about the weather, politics, and current events. It is a type of benign babble that leaves everyone involved with a sense of empty accomplishment. It serves no real purpose other than an indifferent affront to human intelligence.

If someone should talk Yak-Yak to the Crazy-Master it is almost as if the person were speaking another language. Yak-Yak verbs and nouns all sound the same to the Crazy-Master.

He's never taken the time to learn the language because he's never had a reason to do so.

He interprets most Yak-Yak as voluntary verbal vomit; it is the kind of noise that induces one into a listless trance of indifference and sickening slumber. Don't be fooled by its innocent exterior, what lurks below is nothing short of the devil himself---urging the humdrummer along---into an abyss of dull sewing circles, tea parties, and "sharing" support groups.

> *Perhaps to be sane*
> *in this society is the best*
> *evidence of insanity.*
> *-Addison Gayle, Jr.*

Are you a Yak-Yakker?...

Do you speak when you have nothing to say? Are you uncomfortable with prolonged silences during conversation? If a person endlessly prattles on about nothing, do you politely encourage such wasteful behavior with appropriate eye contact and nods?

Most Yak-Yak is a surface solution to a much deeper problem than simply having nothing to say. Most Yak-Yak is a result of having nothing interesting to do. For example, if a person's life revolves around the plots of television shows and hyperbole found in most tabloid magazines, do you really think such behavior is going to stimulate thought provoking questions and reflections?

People who love life and who live according to the Principles of Crazy-Wisdom have no time or patience for Yak-Yak. Yak-Yakking to a Crazy Master is like offering a King a hot dog at an elaborate feast. He has no use for such garbage. At a feast, the King accepts only the finest foods. And at the feast of life, the Crazy-Master only accepts the finest conversation.

Wisdom is itself a kind of madness.
-John P. Dolan

Why become a Yak-Yak connoisseur when you can dine on some of the finest thoughts this world has to offer? Anywhere you go there are bound to be Crazy-Masters as desperate for fine discussions as you are. Find these people now! Treat all meaningless chitchat like the mental bacteria that it is and stand up to the burgeoning battalions of babble like a mighty warrior of Truth. Put on your Crazy-Master costume and win the battle against this subtle poison. Your Crazy-Master-Mind is dependent on it.

Insanity is hereditary---you can get it from your children!
-Sam Levinson

18. THE INSANE GUIDE TO PECK-PECK CRITICISM...

How does the Crazy-Master do it? How does he live his life with so much joy, happiness and cheerful freedom? There is only one answer: He does not allow the petty manipulations of other people's neurotic derangement to touch his innermost depths. The Crazy-Master moves about the world like an eagle flying over a chicken coop. He does not concern himself with the petty pecking and back stabbing of the silly chicken concerns, he has too many interesting things to see up in the air.

The Crazy-eagle-Master can empathize and minister quite effectively with other people. His Crazy-Wisdom endows him with an acute intuition that enables him to accurately comprehend the profundity of other people's innermost feelings. But what he does not do is get emotionally hooked by skillful chicken manipulators and deviant peck-peck experts. He offers his assistance and guidance when needed but refuses to fall prey to the incessant peck-peck nonsense of another chicken's neurotic sickness.

> *Show me a sane man and I will cure him for you.*
> *-Carl Gustav Jung*

The peck-peck critic...

There is a completely insane segment of our society called professional critics. If they win a million dollars in the lottery, they'll complain that they didn't win two. If they are surrounded by friends and loved ones, they'll complain about the one person that twenty-years ago wouldn't open a door for them at the supermarket. Professional critics have something to say about everything and most everything they say is bad. They are not very happy people and become infuriated with those that are. If the sun is out they will be the first to inform us about rain. If it is raining, they'll tell us all about the hurricane that's on the way.

Professional critics are bad news. They are usually the first to laugh at the antics of the Crazy-Master and the most persistent in their mockery. They will follow the Crazy-Master wherever he goes for the sole purpose of squashing his enthusiasm and personal power.

Watch out for this psychological poison. Some professional critics are very good at what they do because it's really all they've ever done. They are completely miserable unless everyone else is miserable too. They do everything in their power to make their misery contagious.

Treat these silly creatures with great compassion and care. They have not yet learned the ways of the Crazy-Master and are in desperate need of inspiration. They are very often a result of years of negative, hopeless conditioning and demand great delicacy and tact for their removal out of your life.

Getting rid of the peck-pecks...

You don't get rid of a peck-peck, you simply become the kind of Crazy-minded-eagle-Master that flies way above their mindless, petty peck-peck concerns. If a peck-peck pecks away at your enthusiasm when you mention a particular dream or desire---remember that he or she is a chicken---and chickens can't understand the dreams of an eagle. Chickens peck and eagles soar. Chickens cackle in the coop while the eagles glide into their possibilities. You can't expect support and understanding from the chickens because they have no idea what you're doing. They live in a different world than the Crazy-Master. It is often very frightening to them if one of their confreres should choose to fly the coop. It shakes up their world too much to see the possibilities of a Crazy-Master mind at work. It puts their own lives in an uncomfortable light; a light which reveals their own hopeless and hapless hypocrisy.

The way it is now, the asylums can hold the sane people, but if we tried to shut up the insane we should run out of building materials.
-Mark Twain

19. THE INSANE GUIDE TO COMPASSION...

What most people call charitable compassion the Crazy-Master calls "enlightened self-interest." Humdrummers believe they are good because they do good things. The Crazy-Master *knows* he is good not because of the things he does but because of the person that he is.

The humdrummer may get good feelings when he helps an elderly woman cross the street. He will say to himself, "Look at me! I am a kind and charitable young man because I took time out of my busy schedule to help this less fortunate old woman across the street!" Humdrummers equate their external good deeds with interior *sanctity and goodness* and confuse their *outward demonstrations* of ego-gratifying charades with inward charity and altruism. But for the Crazy-Master, nothing could be further from the truth.

He would never equate his "doing" a good deed with his "being" a good person because he knows even an untrained monkey can help an elderly woman across the street.

Compassion and charity are extremely important attributes for the Crazy-Master life but they are not things he does before he awakens, they are things he does *because* he is awake. If he wants to be good then he must first wake up to the goodness already within. If he wants to do compassionate things he must first be the compassion that he already is. Good actions do not make good people but good people always do things that are good.

We mean well and do ill, and then justify our ill-doing by our well-meaning.
-Emerson

Humdrum compassion...

Do you like it when other people see you doing good deeds? Does it make you feel charitable and benevolent to be seen putting twenty-five dollars in the church donation basket? Most people love to be thought of as generous and kind. Most people enjoy the feeling they get when they do something good. Isn't it natural to want to feel those things?

As you can probably guess, the Crazy-Master is not "most people." He does not do good things that make him feel "good" about himself because as long as there is a "self" doing the action---there is no true and lasting goodness that can be derived from what he does.

The usual distinction between sanity and insanity is a false one. We are all insane; the difference between Napoleon and a madman who believes he is Napoleon is a difference in degree, not in kind; both are acting on a limited set of assumptions.

-Colin Wilson

What is a good act?

What is so good about an action that you "know" to be good? If you are doing something because you consciously realize, "I am doing a good thing"---what makes your action any different from someone refraining from a bad action because he is consciously knows it to be bad? In other words, if an action is motivated by a desire to somehow gain pleasure for the self, (i.e. a good feeling for doing something good or not doing something bad), how can the humdrummer get to a place where his actions are totally self-less and un-premeditated? How can the humdrummer work from the perspective of being a good person who naturally does good things instead of being a humdrummer who does good things because it makes his "humdrum self" feel good when he does them?

First off, I am not suggesting that *all* humdrum good deeds are ego-serving and selfishly motivated. But it is important that we realize where many of our deepest intentions lie. It is not enough to do good things and leave it at that. The Crazy-Master must BE a good person by continually examining his interior intentions and motivations. If the humdrummer helps an old woman across the street and says to himself, "Look how good I am, I'm helping an old woman across the street!"

114

What makes the action so good? Who is really benefiting from the help? The old woman? She's just getting across the street. The humdrummer is getting the benefit of being thought of as a good person. Which would you rather have?

If the Crazy-Master life appeals to your innermost self then you must go to your innermost self and examine it with great attention and awareness. If you want to change---then you must become aware of your reasons for wanting to change. Do you want to be a Crazy-Master or do you just want to be crazy? Going deeper into your motivations will bring you closer to your answers---and in the end, it will bring you closer to your truth.

O crazy mind
for this reason I have not
become mad: I haven't
found a madman up to
my wishes. I haven't found
any such madman. Only
false madmen everywhere
True madmen nowhere.
-Baul Song

20. THE INSANE GUIDE TO FINANCIAL INDEPENDENCE...

The Crazy-Master is rich beyond all measure. It does not necessarily mean that he has more money than everyone else but it does mean he has more appreciation for what money he does have. The Crazy-Master can feel more abundant and financially solvent with eight nickels in his pocket than the ordinary humdrummer feels about having eight thousand pounds of gold sitting in some back-room vault. The Crazy-Master can feel rich living in a shoe box because he knows it's not the size of the castle he lives *inside* that counts---but the size of the castle living inside him.

True wealth for the Crazy-Master is enjoying vast riches without being rich. It is understanding the power of *crazy-abundance* without having any dependencies on other people or institutions for financial support.

What is crazy-independent abundance?

Are you financially independent? Can you experience the value of quality living apart from the marketing efforts of our consumer oriented society? Most humdrummers can sustain themselves for a day or two outside of the commercial mayhem of our mass culture---but any more time after that will cause them to feel cut off and alienated from their community at large. They are so addicted to wanting more and more and more that they have completely lost sight of what gifts they have already got.

I have never heard of anyone stumbling on something sitting down.
-Charles Kettering

Crazy-independent abundance is not having money, it is having freedom from having money. If you constantly feel like you need more money, then you will never have enough. Even if you get a million, trillion dollars you will still want more. Because it is not the money you want, it is the wanting you want. Wanting more money is like wanting to fill an eight ounce glass with twelve ounces of water---it is a waste of Crazy-Master energy!

The Crazy-Master is content with what he's got and as a consequence he is given more than he could ever need. He enjoys the simple pleasures of this vast abundant storehouse of unlimited goods and has a wonderful time enjoying their never ending supply.

There is more than enough...

The Crazy-Master has everything he could ever want. No matter what he has, if it's what he got then it's what he wants. The Crazy-Master takes what he gets. If he gets a limousine he takes it. If he gets nothing he takes that too. He uses this attitude in every aspect of his existence. He knows that life is taking what you get and then wanting what you've got. If he gets what he doesn't want it means that he wants something other than what he's got. It sounds like a semantical distinction, but it is really the Crazy-Master's entire philosophical perspective on emotional detachment.

> *Insanity is often*
> *the logic of an accurate*
> *mind overtaxed.*
> *-Oliver Wendell Holmes*

21. THE INSANE GUIDE TO EMOTIONAL DETACHMENT...

Holding on to nothing, the Crazy-Master gets everything. Sounds ridiculous, doesn't it? *It is ridiculous*---but that's how the Crazy-Master life works. The Crazy-Master is emotionally detached from all the petty ego-desires and needy compulsions that drive most humdrummers into their humdrum despair. Nothing can upset the Crazy-Master because he is not set-up to be up-set. He cannot be de-pressed when things go wrong because he is never im-pressed when they go right. One thing is as good as another for the Crazy-Master. He takes life as it comes and comes to life ready to give up what he took.

What can be stolen from the person who owns nothing? What harm can come to him who is too crazy and too free to identify with the things of this world? The Crazy-Master may have palatial castles and fine cars but they are not his. Sure, they may be under his name and he may have them in his immediate possession---but what does that mean? Life is on loan to every person. What he or she acquires in the meantime are passing illusions that have no bearing upon on his or her emotional well-being.

Someone steals the Crazy-Master's new car? So what! It was never his in the first place. Someone mocks and ridicules the Crazy-Master's new blue shoes? So what! His self-worth is not in his shoes any more than the humdrummer's petty concerns are in real life. Cars can be stolen, houses can be robbed, and new shoes can be scuffed. But what happens to the Crazy-Soul who identifies with nothing? Nothing happens! He becomes the observer of life's misfortunes instead of the victim. He is never identified with anything outside his own interior locutions and as a result lives a carefree and happy life.

Imagine what a joy it would be to be free from the cravings and addictions of the humdrum soul? Imagine the possibility of not needing any *thing* or any *one* in order to live life with freedom, passion and delight? This is how the Crazy-Master lives every day. He is like the wind that passes over the ruffled, stormy waters. He is untouched and unscathed by the torment of the humdrum movement below. His life is free from suffering because there is no *identifying self* to receive the suffering.

> *The world is so full of simpletons and madmen, that one need not seek them in a madhouse.*
> -Goethe

Where are your identities

What makes you happy? Are you happy when your favorite team wins? Are you happy when your name gets into the newspaper? What happens when these things don't happen? Are you immediately upset because the airline lost your luggage? Are you impatient and nervous during stressful situations?

The Crazy-Master lives his life simply, free from the emotional dependencies from any of the things or situations of this world. He is liberated from the emotional tugs that govern and manipulate the humdrummer into an affective see-saw of externally induced reactions of happiness and sadness.

If the humdrummer is sad it is because his favorite ball team lost the pennant. If he is happy it is because his favorite team has just won. Humdrummers are like tiny puppets stuck to a ball of yarn. If the ball rolls one way then the humdrummer rolls right with it. If the ball goes another way then he is emotionally caught up in that movement as well.

> *My worldly wisdom is gone,*
> *all call me mad; let them call me*
> *whatever they please; let me get*
> *my mad Mother at the end.*
> *-Ramprasad*

How does your life measure up to the humdrummer? Does your happiness depend upon outside influences and conditions? Do you need favorable circumstances to feel strong, confident and secure? What happens if those circumstances are taken away?

The Crazy-Master is the freest specimen upon this planet because he is not dependent upon anything on this planet for his emotional and psychological needs. He does not identify with anything outside himself for support and guidance---and as a result he lives an amazingly enjoyable life.

And what is an authentic madman?
It is a man who preferred to become mad in a socially accepted sense of the word, rather than forfeit a certain superior idea of human honor... For a madman is also a man whom society did not want to hear and whom it wanted to prevent from uttering certain intolerable truths.
-Antonin Artaud

22. THE INSANE GUIDE TO BEING EMOTIONALLY DETACHED...

Emotional detachment is not something the Crazy-Master acquires through hard work or struggle. Rather it is the gradual realization of the illusory nature of the humdrum desires and concerns of the normal, every-day humdrummer mind. It is not something he gets after many years of continued effort and exertion, it is something he wakes up to and discovers that it's what he's had all along.

The Crazy-Master begins his emotional detachment by first giving up ownership of everything he has ever acquired for at least one month out of his life. He does this for two reasons. One: he has to give it all up eventually---so why not sooner than later. It will relieve the Crazy-Master of the humdrum emotional trials and worries about having to protect, insure and safeguard so many "things" that have no real bearing on his spiritual and psychological well being. Two: it is a reminder to the Crazy-Master how much he can actually do without.

What does the Crazy-Master really need? Two houses? Three? Twenty? Does he need three cars? How about the latest computerized technology for his dishwasher? Does he really need all of the things our consumer oriented society persuades him that he must have?

I am not saying any of these things are bad. In fact, many of them are very good. It is only when we confuse these "things" with our deepest heart's desire that we become apprehensive and sel-absorbed.

We all agree your theory is crazy; what divides us is whether it is crazy enough to be correct.

-Niels Bohr
Commenting on a proposal regarding the ultimate nature of matter

Giving it all up...

There are many ways to approach this Crazy-Master challenge. One way is to take all your belongings and put them in storage for a month. You can use a friend's garage or rent out some space at a storage facility in your area. Or if you are even a little more daring than that, you can take everything you own and put it all in your front yard with a sign that reads: I AM SIMPLIFYING MY LIFE. PLEASE TAKE WHATEVER YOU WANT. I know this sounds like a radical step---but the Crazy-Master is a radical being. It takes a crazy-courageous soul to become emotionally detached from the humdrummer things of this world.

Who are the madmen, in God's name? Those who wonder about it or the others? If we ever began to speak about it out loud, what would they do with us, tell me?

-Victor Serge

128

When I was twenty-three and preparing to move into the seminary at the University of Notre Dame, I invited fifteen friends over for a brunch. After we ate, I invited them all to go through my apartment and take whatever they wanted. I kept about two or three boxes of personal belongings---but for the rest, I gave it all away.

Most people thought I was nuts for doing this. At the time I had over one thousand books, tons of clothing, furniture, and all kinds of little things one collects over the years. It was a collection of everything I had owned over the course of my twenty-three years of existence. It was all of my life in one apartment and all of my belongings that I most treasured. Why did I give them all away? I still don't know. And for some reason it doesn't matter that I don't know. It seemed to make perfect sense at the time---and to this date I have a sense of liberation from "things" that I never thought I could possibly have.

> *Logic does not exclude*
> *madness.*
> -Eric Fromm

Being detached...

I still don't have many "things" in my life. I live in a small room with a hammock, I have enough food to eat for a week or two at a time, and I even have a little motorcycle to get around on. I have a few books, a guitar, and a handy little computer for my writing projects. I have a couple pairs of pants, two or three tee-shirts and a nice dress shirt for special occasions. My personal journals and notebooks make up the majority of my possessions, and overall---I could fit all my "stuff" in the back seat of a small car.

Now, I am not recommending that you or anyone else live as I do. I live the way I live because it suits me to do so. I don't have many physical possessions but I feel like the richest guy in the world. Maybe you want a twenty thousand square foot mansion and a yacht. Maybe you want a butler and a limo driver. Who knows? Your Crazy-Master mission of madness may lead you to places of unlimited wealth and fortune. That is what you must find out for yourself.

Your attachment to detachment...

Being detached from the world does not mean giving up your possessions. It means giving up your illusions of a personal worth that is tied up with your possessions. Maybe you own many things. Maybe many things own you. No one knows better than yourself. If the detachment challenge makes you crazy then maybe those feelings of craziness are worth examining more than anything else. The key is not getting rid of every thing---it is getting rid of every illusion. Humdrummers have so much that they rarely have the time to attend to even one thing in particular. They have everything in the world except the awareness of the world they have. That is why it is important to be free from things. It gives the Crazy-Master time, patience and awareness to appreciate the one "thing" that is most important. And that one thing is what you must discover.

The question is not yet settled, whether madness is or is not the loftiest intelligence--- whether much that is glorious--- whether all that is profound---does not spring from moods of mind exalted at the expense of general intellect.
-Edgar Allan Poe

PART TWO:

The Magic

Of The Crazy-Master

23. THE INSANE GUIDE TO FAITH...

Crazy-Master-Faith is the most important step to becoming an authentic Crazy-Master. It is the last thing that separates the Crazy-Master from all of the other masters of the world and gives him the extraordinary capacity to make astonishing things happen within his own life.

If living a uniquely magnificent life appeals to your innermost crazy-conscience, then this portion will serve you well. Everything in this book has been leading you to this point. Read this section carefully, it is longer than the other sections because it serves as a backbone for everything you've already learned. These are the foundational keys to all Crazy-Master perspectives and the foundational spirit from which you'll find your Crazy-Master life!

Quit now, you'll never make it. If you disregard this advice, you'll be halfway there.
-David Zucker

Do you have Crazy-Master-Faith?

Are you crazy enough to believe that you could move a mountain? Could you say to Pike's Peak, "go on, move over there!" and then watch as it miraculously moved? How about a small hill? Or how about earning $50,000 in three months? Or in two weeks? Do you have the faith to create the impossible? Jesus said we can have whatever we wish so long as we are crazy enough to wish for it. He said all we have to do is to say to the mountain, "move from here to there," and it would do so. Are you crazy enough to believe something like that?

Most people claim to be Christians but laugh whenever I pose that question. They say things like, "Jesus was the son of God, of course he could move a mountain!" But what they fail to realize is that Jesus never took credit for any of the miracles he enacted, he always attributed his miraculous powers to the power of a person's *faith.* "Your faith that has healed you," he said many times after healing an infirmity---

"anything is possible for anyone who has faith"(Mk.9:23). Now this is a strange thing for Jesus to say, possibly the strangest thing Jesus *could* say. He not only pulled himself out of the "wonder-worker" role that most people assume only applies to him---but he also brought the individual person up to a whole new level of responsibility.

TO SABOTAGE HIS COMPETITION, VINCENT WOULD STAND OUTSIDE ANTONIO'S BARBER SHOP, AND GASP IN HORROR AS HIS CUSTOMERS WALKED OUT.

It is no longer acceptable for human beings to suffer! That was Jesus's crazy-transformational message. We have the power to heal our own inner selves, to awaken the sleeping Crazy-Master within and live our lives with passion, cheerfulness and joy. That is why so many people loved him!

He lived the Crazy-Faith message to its fullest extent and showed everyone else how they could do the same.

How to "get" the Crazy-Master-Faith...

There is no way to "get" Crazy-Master-Faith. It is not "wishful thinking" or "pleading with God." It does not lie in the strength of your conviction or even in the positivity of your thinking. Faith simply is a *way* of looking at the world. It is not "wishing" you could move a ten-trillion ton mountain, it is looking at the mountain and *knowing* it will move! Obviously, moving a mountain will take enormous amounts of Crazy-Master-Faith---but think of the possibilities that the power of faith can have in your own life.

Two wrongs don't make a right,
but they do make a good excuse.
-Thomas Szasz

What if you could turn around your financial situation or send all your children to college without any loans? Imagine having the power to change your destiny instantaneously or being able to eliminate a life threatening disease in a matter of seconds? You can do it! How can you do it? You can do it because Jesus did it and he said that you can do the same. What other reason do you need? Why not give it a try? You've got nothing to lose. Whether you are a Christian, Jew, Buddhist or Scientologist---you can inherit this unique power and use it in your own life.

> *Men are so necessarily mad,*
> *that not to be mad would make a*
> *madman of another order of*
> *madness.*
> -Blaise Pascal

How to inherit this power...

The power of faith is nothing more than the belief that good prevails over evil. It is looking into every dire situation with the feeling that "even this can be overcome." How can you get this feeling? Very simply. If you look at a horrible situation and can't find any good in it---look harder. There is always something good. Always. Your house got robbed and all of your valuable possessions were taken? Most humdrummers would say, "How horrible!" But you are not a humdrummer. You are not satisfied with the response, "How horrible!" There was a reason for this disaster and the reason is a good reason. Maybe you have to simplify your life and this was the universe's way of showing you how. Maybe you needed to become more detached from your belongings? Who knows? But that is what you must find out. You must find the good in everything. And if its not there at first glance, you must have the faith to keep on looking.

> *Let us all be mad for the love of Him who was called mad for our sakes.*
> *-St. Theresa of Avila*

The second step is to take whatever good you find and focus on it until it has successfully expanded into every fiber of your being. For example, if you have been diagnosed with stomach cancer and focus upon nothing but the cancer itself---then your faith in the cancer is what will expand, generating fear and helplessness as a result. But if instead, you allowed this news to stimulate moments of creative reflection and intuition---then perhaps your faith in other things might expand in place of the cancer. Perhaps you hate your job and the undue stress it causes in the center of your gut. Perhaps you needed the cancer to grow in order to remind you of what's most important for you in your life. This insight could lead you to discover faith in other things, such as leisure time for your soul or training in a different vocation.

The point is to remember that faith is not some silly wishy-washy response to concrete problems, it is a small step that will set the stage for your larger steps ahead. Your mountains and hills will be moved at your command. But you need a Crazy-Master vision to make it really happen...

When a man says he is Jesus or Napoleon...or claims something else that seems outrageous to common sense, he is labeled psychotic and locked up in the madhouse...
Freedom of speech is only for normal people.
-Thomas Szasz

24. THE INSANE GUIDE TO VISION...

Clarity of vision is the key to making crazy, head spinning miracle-dreams come true. If the Crazy-Master-miracle-dream is real to the Crazy-Master then it will only be a matter of time until it is real to everyone else as well. People will call him crazy for believing in such ballyhoo---but as always, it is the Crazy-Master in the end, who eventually demonstrates the insanity of everyone else.

Madness need not be all breakdown. It may also be break-through. It is potential liberation and renewal as well as enslavement and existential death.
-R.D. Laing

A *few suggestion's for beginning dreamers...*

Beginning to dream is like learning to see in the dark. At first, your eyes see nothing. The darkness is too overwhelming for your saturated eyes and you spend a few minutes feeling around for objects and people. But after a moment or two, your eyes begin to adjust. You see things that you hadn't previously noticed and within the envelopment of darkness you begin sensing a whole new world of objects, people, and circumstances.

Turning dreams and visions into reality is like adjusting your eyes to the initial darkness. You must have patience and faith that our dreams are as real the moment we think about them as they are when they come to fruition. Everything before you now was once a dream to *someone* in the past. Who is to say your dreams in the present will not be the realities for yourself in the future? There is only one person who can say that and that person is you.

If you're not crazy enough to believe in your dreams right now then no one else will be either. No one is going to get behind your eyeballs and start driving around your life unless you start driving that life yourself. No one will care where you go until you start caring for yourself!

> *Mumbling and prattling*
> *the many names...while onlookers*
> *say, "They're crazy!" entering in*
> *and not entering cities, standing*
> *still or swaying before a laughing*
> *world they dance, they leap*
> *undone by feeling and the gods*
> *bow down before them.*
> -Ramanujan

You got a dream? You got something you want to do? Then you must do it! YOU MUST DO IT! You have no confidence? You have no contacts? No money? No ideas? Great! More fuel for the Crazy-minded-Master. People will call you crazy. They will laugh at you and tell you to stop wasting your time. They will mock your every step and tease you behind your back. But that kind of response can be very good. It can indicate that you are driving your life against the flow of humdrum traffic---and all the other put-put go-carts are getting a little nervous watching this crazy speedster driving in the other direction.

Never underestimate the power of human stupidity.
-Robert Heinlein

Put-put-humdrummers get nervous about anything that goes against their narrow, silly world view. If you see a SLOW vehicle or two cursing at your "reckless" driving, then give yourself a little more acceleration. Don't mind the put-putters---by the time they realize where you're going, they'll be too far behind to ever catch up!

Don't worry too much about being laughed at. Every great visionary starts out as a laughing stock. Just do something, ANYTHING---that will make this dream happen. It all begins as a thought and ends with your actions. Your dreams can become real---only you must be crazy enough to believe in them!

25. THE INSANE GUIDE TO MIRACLES...

Humdrummers believe that all miracles are super-natural events that mysteriously contradict the "laws of natural science." They believe such unusual acts to be "unexplainable" events in the course of human understanding and comprehension. But for the Crazy-Master, "laws of nature" are nothing more than modern intellectual constructions. For him, no such laws even exist. In fact, up until a few hundred years ago there were no "laws of nature." Miraculous events were simply more strange, wondrous addition to an already very strange and wondrous world. Inexplicable "miracles" were not looked upon as contradictory to human intelligence, because as far as our ancestors were concerned, the entire living universe was an inexplicable miracle to human intelligence. It is only our modern day humdrum "intelligence" that arrogantly assumes that our " theoretical laws" have figured everything out. Our laws have done nothing of the kind. We have a lot of ideas about how things work and many of them are very accurate. But in many ways we are as ignorant of universal truths as were our ancestors. There is still wide-spread unhappiness and misery despite our advances in the natural and super-natural sciences. The only difference is that we have found more impressive words to conceal and perpetuate our ignorance.

All of us are mad.
If it weren't for the fact every
one of us is slightly abnormal,
there wouldn't be any
point in giving each person a
separate name.
-Ugo Betti

The humdrum ho-hum is amazed with the silliest things. For example, show him ordinary water that turns into extraordinary wine and he'll grow ecstatic with excitement. But show him instead how ordinary wine can turn into an extraordinary communal drink between friends and he'll have trouble keeping his sleepy eyes open.

The normal person cannot find the miraculous in the common and he consequently becomes blinded to all else. He will be astonished to see a dead man brought back to life without ever having investigated the possibilities of his own existence! That is why the Crazy-Master doesn't believe in super-natural occurrences---because for him, every occurrence is super-natural! Every event brings its own miraculous wonderment. And that's what makes the Crazy-Master so crazy: he can't get over how insanely magical this world is!

Where are your miracles?

Extraordinary miracles are hidden within the ordinary miracles we see every day. And we shall never create extraordinary miracles in our ordinary lives until we have attained an awareness of the extraordinary miracles we already are. Can you see yourself in this way? Humdrummers want a "miracle" cure for cancer without ever investigating the miracles such cancer may have brought.

Cancer in and of itself, is not an evil creation. Cancer is an effect of a certain type of cause. If one's spiritual body is neglected then one's physical body shall suffer the corresponding consequences. But instead of inquiring into the gifts of our miraculous cancer, the humdrummer wants it immediately removed. He wants a "miraculous occurrence" without an understanding about the miracle that has already occurred.

I have a friend who grew cancer as a response to his hectic, stress-filled life. "I hated my job and my living situation," he once told me, "it was like getting kicked in the gut once I found out about the cancer. I felt as though my life was flushing itself down the toilet and the cancer was the last flush. It really got me to re-think things and see why my existence was barely enjoyable. I wish I could have realized

147

the lesson some other way, but this is how things unfolded for me."

He has since had several successful treatments and is doing remarkably well. He quit his job, moved out of the city, and is now working as a free lance artist in the mountains of North Carolina. It took almost losing his life for him to realize what life he had. In a strange way he almost needed the "unhealthy" cancer to make his existence healthy.

Life is a shit sandwich.
But if you've got enough bread,
you don't taste the shit.
-Jonathan Winters

Think about it, where does cancer come from? Is it not the body's imaginative response to our soul's lack of creativity? Is it not an expression through our body that has not been allowed expression in our lives? Most stomach cancer is gotten from eating fatty, salty foods. Why do we eat such unappealing non-nourishment? The body doesn't want it so why do we eat it? The Crazy-Master suggests it is a lack of creative inspiration. When we have neglected the care of our body then the care of our soul is neglected as well. And in the light of such neglect, the soul craves attention in some other form---even if the form is cancerous and deadly.

Most of us cling to "sanity" with a steel grip. Does fear of being regarded by others as insane confine us to a cage of responsible behavior that limits freedom and cripples our ability to love? And is it in fact such a wonderful thing to be regarded as sane?
-Jim Forest

How to widen our creative inspiration...

The miraculous is all around. All we need to do is to open our eyes to see it. The Navajos have an opening in the roof of every home in order for them to see the sky from every angle. They don't do this because they feel a need to waste heat, they do it because they honor the sky as a sacred dimension of an already sacred and miraculous world. When we are able to perceive our world in such miraculous dimensions---we shall be ready for the crazy-miracle creation in our own lives...

The world is becoming like a lunatic asylum run by lunatics.
-David Lloyd George

26. THE INSANE GUIDE TO CREATING YOUR FIRST CRAZY MIRACLE...

Miraculous creations are Crazy-creations because they come from a place that is beyond the sane, rational rubrics of everyday thinking. It is a place beyond common sense intelligence and reasonable logic. It is a place most people never even acknowledge as important because they are too busy complaining about all the things they *don't* have.

In order for the Crazy-Master to create a miracle, he must first be grateful for the miracles he already has. He must honor his body as the divine vehicle that it is. He must bow down before this earth as a sacred house of miraculous gifts and gratuities. He must envision his life in a new dimension of immense possibilities and potentialities. He must discard all conventional, limiting modes of thought and open his mind to the limitless abundance that exists all around.

What does this mean in practical terms? It means the Crazy-Master must become a little crazy. He must be thankful for the things that most people take for granted. He must love and honor those people, places and situations that most normal humdrummers complain and scoff about on a daily basis.

In the past, men created witches; now they create mental patients.
-Thomas Szasz

The power of positive insanity...

First off, you must keep your miracle plan between yourself and maybe one or two other Crazy-Master companions who understand the power of positive insanity. Don't let any of the bored, lifeless humdrummers get their greasy little hands all over your potential creation. Their negativity and pessimism is poison to the Crazy-Master-Miraculous-Mind and can cause you to second guess the plausibility of your vision.

You forget what you possess.
Such is the state when love
comes.
-Lalan

Get yourself a dream board. I have three very large cork boards set up in different spots in my room. They are a collection of pictures and written descriptions of all the things I would eventually like to have and do. It is a sacred place for me. I only place upon it those things that I am truly determined to accomplish---because so far, anything that's gone on the board has come into reality!

And third, get yourself a journal. I am amazed how the discipline of creative journaling has changed my life. Unlike the dream board, absolutely everything goes into my journal! I draw pictures, copy down pages from books, paste in photographs, bottle caps, sea shells, clay ornaments, and just about anything else you can imagine.

I am currently in the process of constructing the world's largest journal. As far as I know it is as big as any journal can get. I am binding it myself with leather and it comes to about five feet wide when opened at the spine! It is the most insane looking thing you can imagine but big dreams *need* big books.

When you've got yourself your dream board and journal you must then prepare for step two...

Step Two: visionary madness...

Visionary madness is the fuel that propels your miracles from your mind into the mind of your creator. Most people don't believe in miracles because they don't see themselves as miraculous. But because the Crazy-Master sees himself as miraculous and knows that his creator can help him create whatever miracles he should desire, he is quite unlike most people.

We cannot unthink unless we are insane.
-Arthur Koestler

How to start...

The best way to start visualizing what you want is to first find out if you really want it. Does your gut ache with anticipation whenever you think about it? Does the mere thought of it keep you awake at night and get you up early in the morning? If so, you are on the right track. If not, don't try this exercise until you've found out what you want. It will not work with lukewarm fantasies, it only works with insanely inspired passions.

Sanity is the playground
for the unimaginative.
-Joop Jean Advertisement

Now that you have your dream in mind. Clarify in exact detail what it would be like to have it. Picture the image in your mind with vivid colors, vibrant sounds, and visceral textures. Make the image large and bright. Feel how crazy the image makes you feel. Embrace the insanity of having this image become real. Taste the madness in your mind. Let your thoughts expand into present moment rapture of having this miracle come to be.

Now comes the fun part. If you had this miracle how would you act? Would you jump for joy? Would you kiss the next ten people you meet? Would you call all your friends and relatives and share your excitement? *Now* is the time to do all these things.

You might be thinking, "I haven't gotten the miracle yet...I'm not going to jump around like an idiot for nothing!" That is the thinking of a mediocre humdrum mind. You are not mediocre, you are a Crazy-Master! And being a Crazy-Master, you believe that all thoughts are things. And being things---they already exist. And if they already exist then you have grounds for celebration! You've created your first miracle!

Every man needs a little madness.
-Zorba the Greek

Now it may take you some time to get used to the idea that miracles are created the moment you imagine them---but for a Crazy-Master this thinking is second nature. Miracles are so intrinsic to his Crazy-Master thought that he is hardly surprised when they effortlessly appear to the rest of the world as well.

Start with little visions...

Don't be dismayed if at first your vision seems too daunting. It will take you time to get used to the idea that your life begins with your thoughts. Focus on attainable goals for practice. Start with little visions until you grow in crazy-confidence for the bigger things. It is an addicting little exercise in possibilities, but absolutely essential for the life of a Crazy-minded-Master.

I suppose it is much more comfortable to be mad and not know it, than to be sane and have one's doubts.

-G.B. Burgin

27. THE INSANE GUIDE TO THE END OF THIS BOOK...

In reading the few preceding pages, you have distinguished yourself as a member of a very small but growing group of crazy-minded individuals---dedicated to the pursuit of impassioned madness and unencumbered insanity. You must be congratulated! You are not like most of the people who walked past this book on the shelf saying, "what kind of garbage will they think of next?" You were crazy enough to buy this book---and what's better than that---you were crazy enough to have actually finished reading it! At this point, your potential madness is infinite. There is no inspiring insanity beyond your reach and no impassioned foolery outside your grasp. The world of the

Crazy-Master is yours for the asking. You must only decide how much of it you want to take!

> *Insanity is a perfectly rational adjustment to an insane world.*
> R.D. Laing

It is an exciting stroll along the untravelled path---with many interesting things to do and see. Don't feel too bad that there are so few people coming along. More will be joining in soon. Impassioned insanity is contagious. People will want to know your secret. But don't be too quick to give this book away---chances are, you'll never get it back. Get a few extra copies and pass them around to your friends. Before long, you'll have your own crazy clan of Crazy-Masters---ready to spread the gospel of insanity to anyone crazy enough to listen!

In closing, I leave you with the wisdom of the immortal, imperishable crazy-minded Crazy-Master of all time, Walt---the wild man---Whitman. I don't know when or why he wrote these words, but my Crazy-Master journey began the moment I heard them:

"Love the earth and the sun and the animals, despise riches, give alms to every one that asks, stand up for the stupid and crazy, devote your income and labor to others, hate tyrants, argue not concerning God, have patience and indulgence toward the people, go freely with powerful uneducated persons and with the young and with the mothers of families...reexamine all you have been told at school or church or in any book, dismiss whatever insults your own soul, and your very flesh shall be a great poem."

Let your poetry speak throughout your life this moment. Become the guiding Crazy-Master for all the world to see and the future sanity of this world will never be the same!

May your madness set you free!

"We all need a little madness to keep from
going insane!"

Leonard M. Foley, III is an avid (one time) skydiver who derived the basis for his Crazy-Master approach to life during his first jump from a single engine aircraft on March 11th, 1992.

He has since sought the tutelage and guidance of some of the most acclaimed Crazy-minded-Masters that the world has yet to know. In his travels he has discovered simply: "Madness is freedom. The freedom to do what you want when you want to do it. If you want to be free then you must be free to do those things that most people are afraid of doing. Most "sane" people neurotically fear the laughter, rejection and scorn of other people. The Crazy-Master laughs at these fears and hence becomes the most courageous specimen on the planet."

Incorporating this philosophy into his life, Mr. Foley left college to start a Hot Air Balloon Company together with his father. He has spent three years studying for the priesthood at the University of Notre Dame and has published three other books. He lives and writes somewhere in Mississippi.